AF800952

INNER VOICES:

AND OTHER ESSAYS ON JUNGIAN PSYCHOLOGY

Robin Robertson

Published in 2017
Manyhats Press
846 N. Monterey Street
Alhambra, CA 91801
rrobertson@pacbell.net

First published in 2013 as a Kindle e-book

Copyright 2013, 2017 by Robin Robertson, Ph.D.

All rights reserved. No part of this publication may be reproduced or transmitted in any form or by any means, electronically or mechanical, including photocopying, recording, or by any information storage and retrieval system, without permission in writing from Manyhats Press. Reviewers and scholarly books may quote brief passages.

Library of Congress Cataloging-in-Publication Data

Robertson, Robin, 1944-
Inner Voices: and Other Essays on Jungian Psychology
by Robin Robertson
Included bibliographical references and index

ISBN-13: 978-0692928899 (Manyhats Press)
ISBN-10: 0692628898

1. Jung, C. G.

Printed in the United States of America

PRAISE FOR ROBIN ROBERTSON'S OTHER BOOKS

Beginner's Guide to Jungian Psychology

The world of consciousness has its spokesman in Robin Robertson. He's becoming a "name brand" when it comes to explaining in fresh terms the important mysteries that lie within us. Use his book as a guide and you'll discover within yourself the buried treasure that already knows your name!

- Psychologist and Writer Henry Reed.

The Shadow's Gift

This is an unusually intelligent and accessible contribution to the 'self-improvement' literature. Robertson is a Jungian-oriented psychologist who demonstrates a profound and personal grasp of the intricacies and benefits of recognizing and engaging with shadow issues. He neither trivializes nor mystifies the power and dynamics inherent in such an engagement and his choice of material to amplify and illustrate his thesis – that the shadow is essential to our wholeness and need not be feared and excluded.

- *Journal of Analytical Psychology.*

At the End of Time: Prophecy and Revelation: A Spiritual Paradigm.

Robin Robertson continues to be one of the best writers about Jungian psychology in contemporary times, exploring complex ideas in clear, straightforward fashion. Yet he never dumbs the material down, respecting the intelligence & curiosity of the reader to follow where he guides. It's just that he has a deceptively conversational prose style that draws the reader in immediately & comfortably, while unfolding one rich & nuance concept after another, and showing how they all connect.

- William Timothy Lukeman, Amazon.com.

Jungian Archetypes: Jung, Gödel, and the History of Archetypes

Dr. Robertson is able to put high-order theory into simple, elegant, comprehensible prose. He is not only good at this; he is genuinely gifted.

- Dr. Michael Washburn, *S.U.N.Y Press.*

Mining the Soul: From the Inside Out

Dr. Robin Robertson is a masterful teacher who weaves the threads of brain research, Jungian psychology, mysticism, meditation and magic in a way that entertains and informs. I found myself utterly intrigued with his unique insight into that pair of opposites: inner and outer. This fine book is for the professional who wants a new and really good tool for his psychological tool kit, and for the lay person who wishes to learn how to penetrate the mysteries of the psyche. Robertson speaks with authority, clarity, humor, and depth.

- Gilda Frantz, Co-Editor, Psychological Perspectives,

Indra's Net: Alchemy and Chaos Theory as Models for Transformation.

Robertson has a deft touch. His descriptions of both alchemy and chaos science are extremely clear. He manages to delineate each discipline clearly without compromising the dignity of either the ancient or modern science. . . . In shot, this is a beautiful and insightful book, and is itself a model of how to make use of science as an analogy to spirituality with integrity.

- Andrew Philip Smith, The Gnostic-3.

Acknowledgments

Grateful acknowledgement is made to both Taylor & Francis and to the Society for Chaos Theory in Psychology for permission to republish the articles previously published in their journals.

Grateful acknowledgment is also made to Princeton University Press for permission to quote material in the *Collected Works of C. G. Jung* within fair use limits.

OTHER BOOKS BY ROBIN ROBERTSON

Jungian Archetypes: Jung, Gödel and the history of archetypes

At the End of Time (3rd ed).

Beginner's Guide to Jungian Psychology

The Shadow's Gift (3rd ed).

Mining the Soul: from the inside out

Indra's Net: alchemy and chaos theory as models for transformation

Jung and Frodo: 7 Paths of Individuation in Lord of the Rings;

Chaos Theory In Psychology and the Life Sciences (co-editor with Allan Combs)

TABLE OF CONTENTS

THE MOTE IN YOUR EYE

In Praise of Projection

Projection is always an indirect process of becoming conscious--indirect because of the check exercised by the conscious mind, by the pressure of traditional or conventional ideas which take the place of real experience and prevent it from happening.

C. G. Jung [1]

There is usually little good said about projection. Critics of projection assume that the person stays trapped in the projection, forever fitting the world to their projections rather than adapting their projections to the world. They believe we are like the robber Procrustes of Greek mythology, who made his victims fit his bed, either by stretching them if they were too short, or cutting off part of their limbs if they were too tall. Eventually Theseus forced the same punishment on Procrustes.

As the above quotation makes clear, Jung saw a deeper purpose in projection: projection leads to consciousness. Projection occurs when consciousness refuses to acknowledge some symbolic expression which is trying to emerge from the unconscious. Eventually the energy of the symbol is so great that it thrusts itself forth into the physical world. [2] Projection is thus a creative attempt by the psyche to resolve the tension created by the shadow problem (or any other stalemated situation between conscious and unconscious). In all relationships, the unconscious selects, from a nearly infinite gallery of inner figures, one particular personality which it chooses to project out onto someone in the outer world. Thus when we're first getting to know someone, most of what we see is a projection of a figure inside us. As we come to know them better, our inner picture comes closer to matching the actual person. But we are always projecting; relationship is an active process of throwing our inner world out onto the outer world, not merely a passive pulling in of the world outside us.

This is already a major difference from the traditional view of our relationship with the outer world, in which we are viewed as passive recipients of sensory stimuli from the world around us. Strict behaviorists (and there aren't many left) would then say that the stimuli automatically lead to responses, without any intervention within. Most psychologists would say that our minds process the information we read from the outer world, in order to come up with the optimum response. But projection presumes something quite different. In order for projection to operate at all, we have to have a highly developed model of the world inside us (and I'm not saying this is necessarily a visual model). Instead of passively accepting new stimuli from the world around us, we continuously project out our best guess as to what we are about to encounter. As long as the stimulus doesn't vary too much from the inner model, we don't have to deal with anything except that inner model. When we encounter something that doesn't fit well with our inner model, our psyche does its best to project something, then scramble to adapt.

So when we are forced by inner pressures to project emotional issues out onto the world, this is merely an extension of a natural process we use in all our engagements with the world. Jung says that "it is . . . not surprising if the unconscious appears in projected and symbolized form, as there is no other way it might be perceived." (3) As we will see later in this paper in discussing perception in more generality, this model of the dynamic between inner and outer reality, is science's best current guess at how we actually do interact with the world.

When we don't deal consciously with emotional issues, those issues gather related experiences around them, to form complexes within the unconscious. Because we are human beings whose emotional lives center around other human beings, inevitably those complexes take on human form, and eventually become autonomous personalities. Once formed those inner personalities appear in dreams and fantasies, wearing a variety of outer manifestations, all of which fit the always vague, inchoate personified form of the complex. We can consciously engage with those figures through working with our dreams, and/or with active imagination. But if we don't make the attempt on our own, the psyche will! It identifies someone sufficiently like the personified complex, to be able to wear the projected identity. Marie-Louise von Franz says that "seldom, if ever, is nothing of what is projected present in the object. Jung speaks therefore of a "hook" in the object on which one hangs a projection as one hangs a coat on a coat hook." (4)

But consider what has happened: the emotional issue, previously abandoned in the unconscious, has now found a way to force itself in front of our eyes, where it can no longer be ignored. And in the process, it has brought along all the emotion tied to that complex. Even if consciousness remains unaware of the inner issue, it is now confronted with the problem as an outer event with which it is forced to deal. Since we see the projection rather than the actual person wearing the projection, we deal with the issue as directly as we would in a dream. And, because we are encountering it in the outer world, there is less possibility of dismissing it or intellectualizing it, as we might do with a "mere" dream. And it carries the whole emotional load of the complex with it, which makes things happen in the outer world.

Psychologist Henry Reed has done research on the connections between intimacy and psi. (5) His general conclusion is that so-called extra-sensory perception is in actuality an extension of the normal process of intimacy. Or to put it another way, our empathy for someone can easily flow still further into territory that supposedly is limited to psychics. Dr. Reed discussed this in terms of a "liminal zone"; that is, the space that lies between two (or more) people. In any interaction between two people there is always a fuzzy place which is neither the one nor the other, but instead is formed by their interaction. We have all felt our own personalities dissolve in the liminal zone that forms with a loved one, or equally with someone we despise. It is in just that fluid place that the possibility for change resides. And projection is the first step into that liminal zone.

Projection is the way the psyche reaches out to someone new. Jung says that "everyone creates for himself a series of more or less imaginary relationships based essentially on projection." (6) Every new relationship--whether with a person, an object, or an idea--in some way involves projection. In order to fall in love, we have to first project our ideal mate out onto someone in the world. That is the only way to generate enough desire to pull us into a new relationship. As our love progresses, the unconscious is forced to adapt to the differences between the actual person and our inner ideal. Hopefully, our projection modifies to fit the person rather than the person being forced to match the projection, as in the Procrustean bed we mentioned earlier. As we come to know the person better, if the fit is too discordant, then the projection falls apart, and the relationship dies. If the fit is too exact, there is no creativity in the process, as we are merely interacting with a previously defined stereotype. When, however, there is a creative tension between the actual person and the symbol being projected, growth occurs. As Jung says "we understand another person in the same way as we understand, or seek to understand, ourselves. What we do not understand in ourselves we do not understand in the other person either." [7]

Projection and Perception: Amazing Animal Stories

The plain truth is that neither in man nor beast are the hemispheres the virgin organs which our scheme called them. So far from being unorganized at birth, they must have native tendencies to reaction of a determinate sort. These are the tendencies which we know as emotions *and* instincts.

William James. [8]

Perhaps we need to step back for a moment and consider projection as a basic process of nature. All perception begins with projection of archetypal contents out onto the physical world. The unconscious stores and processes the perceptions, building complexes around archetypes, such that over time, the complex comes to be projected, rather than the original archetype. Thus we learn to recognize our particular mother and father, sister and brother, to identify which foods we like and which we dislike, which toys are most fun to play with, and so on, ad infinitum. Nor is this process restricted to humans. To the extent that animals are more driven by their instincts than we are, it is even more likely that they perceive the world around them through a maze of instinctual, archetypal projections which unite them with their kin, past and present, in a unified world that is outside distinctions of time and place.

Throughout the many books written by naturalist and zoo-keeper Gerald Durrell, are scattered wondrous stories of the innate abilities of animals. Several concern the intricate nest-building abilities of birds. The tailor-bird, for example, actually sews up a nest, using two leaves, cotton strings which it gets from somewhere unknown, and its beak as a needle. Durrell watched a different bird--a weaver-bird--weave its nest upon a slender branch. It draped strands of palm fiber around the branch, then tied them together to form a weave, which gradually built into a nest. The completed nest was so strong that Durrell could only take it apart with great difficulty, using all of his strength. [9] These birds had to already have the nest-building knowledge stored inside themselves, as it was stored in generations before of their species. When the time came to build a nest, that deep instinctual--archetypal--knowledge guided their behavior totally. They project every step of the nest-building process out onto the world, finding what they need. For example, it can't be explicit to cotton strings, since they might find something totally different that would do just as well. That's the power of projection.

Even more remarkable is a marvelous story he tells about red ants warring on a colony of black ants, in order to steal their eggs. The red ants later return to their own colony with the stolen eggs, hatch them, then make slaves of the newly born black ants. As Durrell sees it, the battle plan of the red ants is every bit as complex as that of a human war. Like humans, they send out scouting parties in advance, who search for possible colonies to enslave. Once found, the scouting parties return to the nest to announce their find. During an actual battle which Durrell watched, the red ants used the pincher technique employed successfully in human battles over the centuries. The red ants advanced on their enemy's colony, then split into thirds, with the middle third attacking directly while the other two thirds encircled the colony. The black ants were too busy fighting the head-on attack to notice their danger until it was too late and they were totally surrounded. This was the same technique that famed nineteenth-century Zulu Chief Chaka used so successfully in his battles with both the British and other African tribes, calling it the "horns of the buffalo."

In this story we encounter all the complexities that are involved with projection. Ants are the supreme example of a collective intelligence, where the individual ants carry a minimum of instinctual knowledge that drives their actions. The behavioral complexity of the colony itself, as in the story above, transcends the instinctual knowledge of the individual ants. The colony is able to go beyond the amount of instinctual knowledge of the individual ants, because of the ongoing interaction between individual ants and their environment. Psychiatrist, mathematician and experimental psychologist William Sulis has speculated that the collective unconscious is itself an example of a collective intelligence that emerges from the interactions of the feeling-toned complexes which it contains. (10)

But our ant story isn't over. When the black ants saw that the battle was lost, they tried to save the eggs, but the red ants were upon them. Here to me is the most astounding of the events. Some of the black ants fought bravely to their death in the defense of the eggs while others, more cowardly (or perhaps more intelligent), laid down their eggs in front of the conquering red ants, and were allowed to survive. It seems incredible that something as relatively unconscious as an ant can make a decision that could be interpreted as either bravery or cowardice. Even an ant can alter its behavior despite being caught within a projection. (11)

Mental Models: How We Come to Categorize the Outer World

Mental facts cannot properly be studied apart from the physical environment of which they take cognizance. . . . our inner faculties are adapted *in advance to the features of the world in which we dwell. . . Mind and world in short have evolved together, and in consequence are something of a mutual fit.*

William James. (12)

In the seventeenth-century, animals were viewed as machines, the brain as a blank slate on which experience wrote its lessons. To explain their seeming life, thinkers such as Rene Descartes actually drew on hydraulics for an explanatory model, largely because the seventeenth-century finally understood fairly well how hydraulic systems worked. By the eighteenth-century, electricity was in vogue for science, so of course electricity was used to explain away life. (13) In our own day, the computer rules supreme so it has become fashionable to view the brain as some sort of super-computer, which comes up with logical solutions to problems. Research into the brain has already revealed this model to be as far away from reality as Descartes' hydraulic model.

Psychologist William James was one of the first to recognize that the brain is in large part a collection of ad hoc solutions to problems. The brain's solutions fit the world because they evolved together. For the same reason, the brains of different species are organized very differently. Brains evolve in order to solve particular problems of particular species. Frogs are interested in worms, so their vision is very worm specific. Humans are most interested in other humans, so our vision is very good at differentiating faces. In each case, the brain is structured to best fit our particular needs.

> *. . . perceptual categorization must both precede and accompany learning. . . . [We live in] an "unlabeled" world--in which the macroscopic order and arrangement of objects and events (and even their definition or discrimination) cannot be prefigured for an organism, despite the fact that such objects and events obey the laws of physics.*
>
> Gerald M. Edelman. (14)

Nobel Prize winning neuroscientist Gerald M. Edelman argues convincingly that the brain must already have structures in place before it encounters the world, but they have to be adaptable structures or it would be impossible to accommodate to the variety that it finds in the world. Accordingly, Edelman views the brain as a selective system which operates much like evolution, rather than as a computational system, or an information processing system. In other words, the brain doesn't have a whole stack of highly structured computational algorithms stored inside it, which it loads much as a computer loads programs. Instead the brain has a huge number of structures that have been selected over time to solve general problems. They may handle the task at hand, but were not necessarily designed to perform the function they actually do perform. So Durrell's nest-building birds contain highly detailed behavioral templates of how to construct their nests. But rather than existing as programs individually stored in separate compartments of the brain, those templates are stored within the brain's structure itself. And the same components that can be used to tell the bird how to build a nest, can adapt to deal with the need for some totally different behavior.

These structures of the brain correspond to Jung's archetypes. How they are used to interact with our environment is, of course, the issue. Here Edelman goes into more detail in essentially describing how archetypes gather complexes around themselves:

> Perception may be provisionally defined as the discrimination of an object or an event through one or more sensory modalities, separating them from the

background or from other objects and events. . . . how, in fact, do we know what an object is? . . . in some sense, the problem of perception is initially a problem of taxonomy in which the individual animal must "classify" the things of its world.

From the standpoint of the adapting organism, the categorization of things is relative and depends upon cues, context, and salience. Categories are not immutable but depend upon the present state of the organism. . . . Animals can nonetheless generalize; that is, an individual organism can encounter a few instances of a category under learning conditions and then recognize a very great number of related but novel instances.

Gerald M. Edelman. [15]

In other words, our perception of the world depends on discriminating one thing from another, then generalizing as necessary. We project out pre-defined categories stored within the structure of the brain, then modify those structures to fit the task at hand. Those modified structures provide us with new categories that are stored within the brains structure, using pre-existing patterns never intended for this particular use. Once stored, they can in turn be projected out onto the world to deal with the same situation in the future.

Let's take a break from the science and think about how this process operates in the psychological projection of personified figures like the shadow or the anima/animus The qualities that these figures possess are already contained within us at an archetypal level. As we refuse to allow aspects of ourselves admittance into consciousness, they gather around the archetypal core into complexes, held together by the emotions we have denied. It is likely that these complexes are actually stored within the brain's total structure, using pre-existing pathways. But that needn't concern us here. What does concern us is the fact that there is a mechanism for adapting archetypal, instinctual knowledge to actual experience. When the energy level gets too high, the figures then get projected out onto the outer world, using exactly the same mechanism we use in all perception. Because we can't perceive any difference between such projections and normal perception, we experience our projection as reality.

Linguist Edward T. Hall argues that we do the same thing with our tools and other extensions of the human body and brain: we confuse the extension with the original function or object which it is extending. Like our cousins, the primates, humans are by nature curious about their environment, and continually try to find ways to extend themselves out into that environment. Tools are the most obvious example. In order to dig tubers out of the ground, we can use our fingers, but if the ground is hard, our fingers can become cut and sore.

Eventually we discover that we can use a stick instead of our fingers: we can dig faster and we don't get sore fingers. The stick has become an extension of our fingers. Because this process is so similar to the concept of transference in psychotherapy, Hall refers to is as "extension transference". In Jung's more general concept of transference and projection, this is a primary method in which the archetype finds expression.

In this regard, Hall is especially fascinated by the work of Russian scientist A. R. Luria. In Luria's *The Man with a Shattered World,* a Russian engineer had brain damage that left him unable to think . . . literally unable to think! However, he still retained much of his vocabulary. Gradually he learned to shift the process of thinking from his mind to paper. In other words, he found, as virtually every writer has found, that he could think something through by writing about it. His unique difference was that this had become the only way he could think. Luria's engineer could now only think on paper; but consider what that implies about how extraordinarily versatile the process of thinking must be. If the process can't operate inside the brain because those parts of the brain no longer work, it can actually use pen and paper as extensions of the brain. (16)

Though Luria's engineer may be an extreme example, it merely points to the active nature of the human thought process. We want to reach out to the world, grasp it, interact with it. The process of projection can thus be seen as one of the most elemental process of the human brain, which makes uses of any medium available for its operation. Throughout this paper, we have tried to show that we approach anything new in life by projecting the world that we already have inside us onto the world outside us. Initially we confuse the actuality with our projection, but gradually we adapt and something new forms inside us which better adapts to reality. Projection is thus a miraculous process that underlies all perception and all change. We should praise projection, not damn it.

REFERENCES

1. C. G. Jung, *CW14: Mysterium Coniunctionis,* 2nd edition (Princeton: Princeton University Press, 1970), par. 486.

2. projection comes from the Latin *projectus,* which is the past participle of *prociere,* "to throw out".

3. C. G. Jung, CW14: Mysterium Coniunctionis, *par. 129.*

4. Marie-Louise von Franz, *Projection and Re-Collection in Jungian Psychology* (La Salle & London: Open Court, 1980), p.3.

5. Henry Reed, "Intimacy and Psi: Explorations in Psychic Closeness", *Journal of Analytical Psychology 41, Part1* (1986), pp. 81-116; "Close Encounters in the Liminal Zone: Experiments in Imaginal Communication", *Journal of Analytical Psychology 41, Part 2* (1986), pp.203-226 .

6. C. G. Jung, "General Aspects of Dream Psychology," *Collected Works, Vol. 8: The Structure and Dynamics of the Psyche, 2nd edition* (Princeton: Princeton University Press, Bollingen Series, 1969), par. 507.

7. C. G. Jung, "General Aspects of Dream Psychology," *Collected Works, Vol. 8: The Structure and Dynamics of the Psyche, 2nd edition* (Princeton: Princeton University Press, Bollingen Series, 1969), par. 509.

8. William James, *The Principles of Psychology, Volume One,* (Unabridged reprint of 1890 edition of Holt and Company) (New York: Dover, 1950), p. 76.

9. Gerald Durrell, *Encounters with Animals* (New York: Avon Books, 1958), pp. 62-66.

10. William Sulis, "Collective Intelligence as a Model for the Unconscious," *Psychological Perspectives, Issue 35* (Los Angeles: C. G. Jung Institute, 1997).

11. Gerald Durrell, *Encounters with Animals*, pp. 74-78.

12. William James, *Psychology (Briefer Course)* (New York: Holt, 1890), pp. 3-4.

13. for much more on the history of views of the brain and mind, see Marc Jeannerod, *The Brain Machine: the Development of Neurophysiological Thought* (Cambridge, Massachusetts and London, England: Harvard University Press, 1985).

14. Gerald M. Edelman, *Neural Darwinism: the Theory of Neuronal Group Selection* (New York: Basic Books, 1987), p. 7.

15. Gerald M. Edelman, *Neural Darwinism*, pp. 26-7.

16. Edward T. Hall, *Beyond Culture* (Garden City, New York: Anchor Books, 1977), pp. 25-40.

SYNCHRONICITY IN A NEW LIGHT

Nature uses only the longest threads to weave her patterns, so each small piece of her fabric reveals the organization of the entire tapestry.
- Nobel-Prize winning physicist Richard Feynmann.

Preludes to Synchronicity at a Halfway Home

I began my training as a clinical psychologist at a "halfway home." It was intended to serve as a temporary support structure for severely disturbed young adults before they could move out on their own. Those who demonstrated their ability to function relatively independently could move into small apartments within a few miles of the main facility. The main facility evidently had a prior existence as a two-story Southern California motel, complete with a now seldom used swimming pool. A central dining room had been added, together with offices for staff and TI's (therapeutic interns, such as I was).

Though the halfway home was located on a large street, it was relatively quiet and isolated by a tall concrete wall which ran entirely along the street side. Other walls enclosed the other limits of the facility. I don't want to make it sound like a prison, as the setting was quite friendly, given the limits on a facility with a relatively small area. You entered through an open doorway cut into the wall on the street, took a right then a left and you were suddenly inside this strange setting. After I had been there for a while and gotten my feet wet, so to speak, I found that as soon as I entered the doorway, before I could see into the facility, I would know if things were "crazy" that day or stable. There was one other therapist, a young woman on the staff, who had the same ability to sense the level of craziness. If I felt a certain queasy feeling as I walked in, I would immediately check with her. She would either confirm that bad things were already happening or, if not, that she felt the same way and was waiting for something to break. And it would--I don't recall our ever being wrong.

Now how did we know that? As best I can express my own experience, the craziness that was struggling to come out of the patients passed inside me. I'm not sure whether the environment was an intermediary carrier or not; I think so. But there were no environmental clues for me to note; rather I felt something inside myself--a "queasiness" as I characterized it above, that I translated into things being crazy outside. Sometimes the young woman or I would say that things "smelled" crazy, which is a common reference to an intuitive feeling. In any case, the key fact is that I had found a gateway that could open even when I was conscious. I experimented further with it.

Note that there is actually research that rats can distinguish a difference in smell between schizophrenics and non-schizophrenics. See Edward T. Hall, The Hidden Dimension (Garden City, New York: Anchor Books, 1969), p. 49. Rats have a much more developed sense of smell than humans, but there is speculation that intuition is an outgrowth of smell. Jung felt that thinking, feeling, and intuition were all outgrowths of sensory perception. Intuition would be a natural outgrowth of smell, thinking out of sight, feeling out of hearing and speech. In my clinical work, I've found that the two main varieties of "craziness" seem to be further outgrowths of a normal predisposition to one or another of these functions. Thinkers become schizophrenic, feelers become manic-depressives.

I started using altered states of consciousness in working with the patients, without any real knowledge of what I was doing--except that it helped. By altered states, I'm not implying anything that most would regard as mystical: if the patient was anxious, I would match my breathing and movements to theirs. When we were in synchrony (which we will discuss much more later), I would gradually slow my movements and breathing, and so would they. Usually the patient would end up in something like a trance state. At that point, if I opened myself to them--there's no other way to express it--I would then find their emotions flowing through me as if they were my own. I would cry their tears, or express their anger. Sometimes, I would have pictures in my mind that weren't from my own life memories. Usually I would find out later that these images were from the patient's life. Often they were symbolic rather than literal. From doing dream work, I was used to translating such images.

Of course, I wasn't always so wise when I experienced feelings that weren't my own. One patient, nicknamed "Red," was extremely paranoid. For some reason, he developed a fixation on me. He would come around the office where the other TI's worked and say nice things about me to them, usually making sure I could hear him. I didn't realize what was going on then, as Red wasn't one of my patients, and I didn't know him very well. In retrospect, I can see that he was developing an intense fear of me, and was trying to win my favor by placating me.

I was pleasant enough to Red since he meant nothing special to me. But his anxiety around me increased. Since this was all coming out of him rather than being an objectively accurate response to a frightening situation, there was probably little, if anything, I could have done to defuse his anxiety. Then one night, when I was outside talking with another patient, Red started shrieking his anger and fear at me from his room. The basic litany was that he knew I was out to get him, but he'd get me first. And he had a knife!

That's a frightening situation for anyone to be presented with. I discussed it the next day in a supervision group with other TI's. They were supportive, but I experienced no relief at all. I became anxious whenever I saw Red, though he now avoided me as much as he had previously sought me out. Soon I was anxious anytime I was at the half-way home, regardless of whether Red was around; everyone began to seem dangerous. I began dreading my visits. I even considered terminating my residency there (as so many other TI's had already done).

Then one day, it hit me that I was experiencing paranoia, just as Red experienced paranoia. I hadn't recognized the symptoms because I had previously had very little paranoia in my own emotional make-up. With no category in which I could put this nameless anxiety I was experiencing, it infiltrated insidiously into my whole outlook on life. As soon as I realized I was experiencing paranoia, the paranoia ceased. The same day, Red had an acute psychotic episode, where he ended up curled into a fetal position and had to be taken to a hospital for short-term treatment. As far as I can determine, Red never even saw me that day. When he returned to the facility several days later, I was a proper therapist again, trying to find some way to help a patient in pain. He and I had no further problems.

Another time, the patient helped me, rather than me helping the patient. I was experiencing an emotional problem, and was in a good deal of pain. The pain was caused because I was stretched between two sides of a moral dilemma and wasn't willing to change my self-definition. I helped myself deal with the pain in the way I usually did at that time: by helping patients deal with their own pain. I was having a session with a patient, who I'll call Jean here. Jean had a very, very hard time articulating. Every word was a struggle because she was constantly experiencing so much emotion--usually anger--that the emotion intervened between her thought and her speech. I had never heard her able to speak clearly about anything, though I had learned that she had depths of perception once I got past her speech problem.

Suddenly, out of nowhere, her speech became startlingly clear, and she told me exactly what I needed to do to resolve my emotional problem. It was like the best therapist/guide in the world was there, who had been listening carefully to my problem, and now gave me exactly the counsel I needed. Of course, I hadn't even mentioned my problem to Jean. As quickly as it happened, Jean was back to her old speech pattern, discussing her issues. Of course, afterwards, Jean knew nothing of what had happened.

Synchrony, Intimacy and Psi

In the field of emotion, which is a phenomenon very much on the border between physiological and psychological reality, rhythm is essential. In states of strong emotion we make rhythmical movements (stamping our feet, for instance) and tend to repeat endlessly the same thoughts and utterances. This led Jung to suspect that unconscious complexes might have a periodical rhythmic nature.

- Marie-Louise von Franz. (1)

Psychologist and dream pioneer Henry Reed has in recent years done similarly pioneering work in psychic connections between people: extra sensory perception. He proposes something that sounds strange only because we think of ESP as strange: that ESP is an extension of normal intimacy between people. Think about that. When we are with a stranger, most of our communication is limited to the content of the words we speak. As in all interchanges between two humans, there is also an unspoken body language that we read unconsciously, but when we don't know someone well, there are definite limits to our ability to interpret the other's actions.

Then imagine two lovers in the early thrall of their love, where they are so intent on each other that the rest of their environment virtually fades from their awareness. They notice anything and everything about their loved one: every movement, every glance is significant to them. If we watch them closely, their actions are like a wonderful dance, part choreographed in advance by the archetype invoked by love and part unique to their pairing. They rarely miss a step in this elaborate dance.

Then think of a long-married husband and wife with a good marriage. Notice just how few words go on there. They understand each other so intimately that each can virtually complete the other's thoughts. They no longer need the intensity of attention of the two young lovers since the other is so embedded within them that they are able easily to function either separately as individuals, or as a pair, each complementing the other to form a whole that is neither one nor the other.

Research by experimental psychologists William Condon and Ray Birdwhistell and by linguistic anthropologist Edward T. Hall demonstrated that this synchronous dance of individuals is more than a metaphor. Filming human interactions in a variety of situations, then viewing them at slowed-down speeds, they were able to watch how tiny, nearly imperceptible body movements by one person cued movements by another. Hall comments that: "viewing movies in very slow motion, looking for synchrony, one realizes that what we know as dance is really a slowed-down, stylized version of what human beings do whenever they interact." This ability to synchronize our movements to our environment "appears to be innate, being well established by the second day of life, and may be present as early as the first hour after birth." (2)

Earlier in this paper I told how I would consciously synchronize my movements and breathing to that of a patient in distress, then guide them into an altered state. In a remarkable example of how this can operate at an unconscious level within a full group, one of Hall's students filmed school children playing in a playground during lunchtime. Though at first viewing of the film, the children seemed to be each "doing their own thing," after repeated viewing, Hall and his student noticed that one little girl was especially active. Over the course of the lunch break, her play took her over the entire schoolyard. The movements of all the other children came in synchrony with her own as she moved into their territory, until the whole group was moving in an unconscious symphony, led by the little girl as conductor. When Hall and his student asked an expert on rock music to watch the film, he was actually able to find a currently popular tune that fit the rhythm so perfectly that once it was "synchronized with the children's play . . . [it] remained in sync for the entire 4-1/2 minutes of the film clip." (3)

Dr. Reed's work starts with this synchrony, then moves beyond into psi. He is a frequent lecturer and workshop leader who uses these occasions to conduct group experiments that benefit both the audience and scientific research. For example, he plays "The Getting to Know you Game" with these audiences. He has a number of varieties of this experiment. In one, a member of the audience, the "agent", reads a nursery rhyme or the alphabet or, more recently, simply counts backwards from 50 to 1. The audience is asked to both concentrate on the voice and observe anything going on within themselves as they listen. Afterwards, they share what went on inside them. "Purely subjective responses show surprising relevance to the objective facts concerning the vocalist's personal life, beyond matters of temperament and mood to facts in the vocalist's environment." (4)

This technique maximizes the information that Dr. Reed can receive and validate. More recently, he has developed several one-on-one variations which maximize the number of people who can be helped by the intuitive insight. In each, he has the audience break into pairs. One variation proceeds as above, with one person counting slowly backwards from 50 to 1, while the other person notices their own stream-of-consciousness. Afterwards, the receiver tells the speaker what they experienced and the speaker tells what does and does not fit their life.

In the "problem response" version, the speaker picks an issue on which they would like to receive advice, but keeps it secret during the countdown. Dr. Reed has found that the listener's response usually provides insight into the problem. Finally, in a "soul retrieval" mode, the listener is:

> Given a format for a story to imagine while traveling on the river of sound of the speaker's voice: go underground, meet an animal helper, find the lost soul fragment of the speaker, heal it and return with it, learning from it what it can contribute to the speaker's life. At the end of the countdown, the listener shares the story with the speaker and gets feedback. This procedure, as simple as it is, with untrained people, strangers as partners, has proven very profound, healing, [calling up] powerful emotional reactions. [5]

I remember participating in a similar experiment at a workshop in Asilomar in 1981, led by a medical doctor and clinical psychologist. He concentrated on a particular variety of psi: psychometry; the ability to access information about a person by physical contact with the person or with an object belonging to the person. He felt that psychometry was a normal ability that anyone could use, one which was especially useful for therapists. Because this was controversial, he came up with a hilarious cover term for the use of psychometry for psychological diagnosis: holographic diagnostic techniques. We each paired up with someone else from the group whom we had never met before. Then we took turns as "sender" and "receiver." The receiver would hold the sender's hand in theirs and concentrate on their own inner process. As a receiver, I remember that I got a picture of a farm house with an old couple. It turned out that the person I was with had, in fact, been raised on a farm by his grandparents!

This was so impressive to me that, when working with patients, I always tried to observe whatever came up in my own mind, remaining open to the possibility that it had something to do with my patient. This works equally well in normal life. I think that we all do this a great deal of the time, reading information about the other person on an unconscious level, then acting on it ourselves with no intervening conscious notice. The process of observing our inner process while engaging in normal interactions with another person at first seems awkward, but itself becomes almost unconscious after a while (if this isn't a contradiction in terms.)

Synchronicity

It is the nature of synchronicity to have meaning and, in particular, to be associated with a profound activation of energy deep within the psyche. It is as if the formation of patterns within the unconscious mind is accompanied by physical patterns in the outer world. In particular, as psychic patterns are on the point of reaching consciousness then synchronicities reach their peak; moreover, they generally disappear as the individual becomes consciously aware of a new alignment of forces within his or her personality.

- F. David Peat [6]

Often we find that gateways open in our lives in ways that don't fit readily into traditional views of reality. Jung coined the term *synchronicity* for meaningful coincidences, occurrences which had significance for us, but for which there is no simple causal explanation. We are all familiar with such events, yet we tend to dismiss them as coincidences, ignoring the fact that it is their meaning for us that seems to trigger them in our lives. For example, thinking of someone and at that moment hearing the phone ring and finding that it is the same person on the phone. Or needing a special piece of information and a book arrives in the mail with just the information that you need. Take a small synchronicity that occurred while working on this material. A fan of a previous book, with whom I had no contact for a year, suddenly wrote me to ask if I could tell her what synchronicity was. Clearly, her interest in synchronicity wasn't what made me write about it, nor was my writing the cause of her interest. The two were separate, yet came together in a way that was meaningful for both of us. How can we explain this (other than, of course, to ignore the fact that it had meaning for both of us and to dismiss it as coincidence)?

In my own life and in the lives of those around me, I have repeatedly found that synchronicities increase in intensity, frequency and clarity at special times. These include times of transition, ceremony, crisis, fear, and other exceptional times: birth, death, marriage, separation, changes in my professional life, etc. Accordingly, when synchronicities begin to appear in my life, I know that something special is afoot, and try to get in touch with those synchronicities, to become more centered, more aware of what the psyche is trying to tell me. When I'm successful with this process, the synchronicities increase in frequency. Psychologist Ira Progoff agrees with this position.

> By definition one cannot *cause* synchronistic events, but on the basis of observations in this area over the last twenty years, it does seem to me to be possible to develop in a person an increased sensitivity to synchronistic events, and especially a capacity to harmonize one's life with such occurrences. [(7)]

When I was still seeing patients in a clinical setting, I found that nearly all my patients went through similar issues at the same time. This was especially noticeable at watershed points in their lives. For example, when after a lot of progress, my first patient of the day was stuck on what, for example, could be loosely termed a father issue (or a mother issue or a variety of others), I knew that I would be dealing with the same issue throughout the day with most of my patients. This was most marked when after being stuck for a long time, one patient suddenly had a break through. It was quite exciting to see a whole series of epiphanies throughout the day. But a similarity of theme that lasted over an extended period of time was the more common synchronicity that I noted. Since I saw patients who varied from very disturbed patients at a halfway home to outpatients in a counseling center, the particulars of the issue would take different form. But then all Jungians are used to seeing the variety of clothes that a symbol wears. In Victor Mansfield's words from his recent book on synchronicity:

> An important implication of acausal connection through meaning is that in *synchronicity the meaning is primary while the objective and subjective events that correlate are secondary and contingent.* (8)

After I had noticed this going on, I went out of my way to remove any possibility that these events were actually causal and that perhaps I was the cause. I would simply note what was going on with the first patient, then stay a bit more detached than otherwise in the early part of a session, so that I wouldn't be feeding the patients cues as to what I expected. In retrospect, I think this was a needless precaution on my part since usually they would come in with the issue plainly on the table. And, of course, it wasn't only my patients that were going through those issues at the same time, so was I. This recognition that what was happening in others might say something to me, and vice versa, was one of the most helpful tools I ever discovered in dealing with this strange unitary world we live in.

Again notice that this required me to discover a previously hidden meaning; i.e., that a patient's issues were not only theirs but mine as well. That in turn caused me to focus more closely on the cycles of emotions and events that we all pass through, either observing others to learn more about myself, or myself to learn more about the situation others were in. There was already a meaning there trying to come out, but it required focus on my part to see it.

As time went on, I began to notice that these synchronicities extended to those with whom I was connected closely in any way, not only those I saw routinely in my daily life, but also those from whom I was separated by distance and only communicated with occasionally. Often very specific types of events would show up across the board. Here I often found that one or another of us might be a few days or even a few weeks behind or ahead of the main group of people, but that seemed only to make this more believable. Synchronicity isn't necessarily simultaneity in time, but simultaneity in inner experience. Time and again, this awareness has enabled me to be able to help someone who wasn't forthcoming with their situation, but who I knew needed help because they were going through something similar to myself and other friends.

> Jung's definition has led to frequent misunderstandings because "coincidence in time" is generally understood as an astronomical simultaneity dependent on clock time. It is rather, a *relative simultaneity,* to be understood as the subjective experience of an inner image coinciding with an outer event. Only in this experience is the time difference abolished, since the event, whether in the past or future, is immediately present. It may happen that inner image and outer event are connected together by an objective, clock-time simultaneity, but that is not the decisive factor. The decisive factor lies in a subjectively experienced, relative simultaneity. (9)

I've also found that synchronicity extends to the inanimate objects that are most significant in my life, especially my car and my computer. Undoubtedly this is an extension of the process I've already been presenting: a pattern emerges in the psyche and bursts forth in some way that grabs my attention and causes me to further focus. So it picks not only the people who are significant in my life, but the objects. I've grown so used to this happening that I'm no longer startled by it. I just stop and look at the event as if it were a dream and interpret it that way. For example, on the few occasions when my car has overheated, it coincided with my pushing myself too hard and not realizing it. My battery never dies when I've got lots of personal energy, only when I'm drifting into depression.

Though I've had many similar experiences with my computer, I remember one event in particular. Several people who were connected with Subud had read a book of mine, contacted me and asked to see me informally. Subud is an esoteric group founded by a Javanese mystic named Bapak Muhammed Subuh. Subuh discovered an inner force, an energy, which could be transmitted to others through a group practice called the latihan (i.e., the Indonesian word for "exercise").

I was working at my computer and had forgotten just when they were going to arrive. Suddenly my computer went crazy, with all sorts of strange symbols racing up and down the computer screen. Nothing I could do would change it, including turning off the computer then rebooting it. Just then the doorbell rang to announce that my visitors had arrived, so I left the computer as it was and went down to meet with them. Their visit turned out to be a very strange and memorable event, though one that ended up having more effect on the life of another friend of mine that it did on my own life. When they had left and I returned to my computer, it had returned to normal and never again duplicated this strange behavior.

For those who think that this might sound like an incipient computer virus, it took place on a little Commodore 64 before destructive hackers bothered with personal computers. The only other time a similar event happened was on another Commodore 64 when lightning struck the wiring of our house. Unfortunately, that poor computer was permanently damaged.

Psychologists Allan Combs and Mark Holland see these physical instances of synchronicity as examples of the Trickster archetype awakening us to something we are overlooking.

> One of the authors likes to refer to such coincidences as "perverse synchronicity."....The key is to relax into the moment, realize that life will not end if the next stoplight turns red, and try to be centered on yourself. Doing this can lead to surprising results. You may find, for instance, that the tricks are actually not so bad. Upon regaining your composure, you often discover that each trick is followed in time by another coincidence that provides a solution to it.

Jung agreed that when the energy in the unconscious was powerful enough, synchronicity could extend to inanimate objects:

> It often seems that even inanimate objects co-operate with the unconscious in the arrangement of symbolic patterns. There are numerous well-authenticated stories of clocks stopping at the moment of their owner's death...Other common examples are those of a mirror that breaks, or a picture that falls, when a death occurs; or minor but unexplained breakages in a house where someone is passing through an emotional crisis. (10)

In his spiritual autobiography, *Memories, Dreams, Reflections,* he gave a personal example. He had been arguing with Freud about such inexplicable, seemingly paranormal events. Just as Freud was leaving, Jung felt a burning sensation in his diaphragm, as if it were a "glowing vault." At that moment, there was a sharp sound from the bookcase, and both turned to it, fearful that it might fall. "There," Jung said to Freud, "that is an example of a so-called catalytic exteriorization phenomenon." When Freud pooh-poohed this as nonsense, Jung told him he was mistaken and said "to prove my point I now predict that in a moment there will be another such loud report." And, of course there was. (11)

This story illustrates the difficulty in finding handy little intellectual boxes in which we can put such events. Did Jung cause the event because he was so heated up by the discussion, so irritated at Freud, that it burst out of him? Then the second time, he actually consciously caused it to happen? Perhaps. Or perhaps, as Jungian analyst Aniela Jaffé suggests, since "Jung was in a highly emotional state . . . his consciousness was drawn, so to speak, into the realm of the unconscious and he was able to 'know' the coming event." (12) How about my patient who turned briefly into my counselor--did my need for help cause her to speak? Perhaps, or perhaps we're in deeper waters than simple causal explanations, even those that involve paranormal causality.

Aniela Jaffe points toward one answer: "one of the main points of Jung's investigations on parapsychology is that *synchronistic events are manifestations of an archetype.* In other words: the archetype is their "organizer." (13)

Notice how similar this is to our relationship to our dreams. We can neither control nor organize our dreams, that organization has to come from within. Though we can't control our dreams, we can become more attuned to them. Even lucid dreams are more like a dialogue with the unconscious than a drama that we are writing from scratch. The process of learning to listen to the psyche is similar, whether we are listening to our dreams or observing the synchronicities that occur in life. In that process, something new emerges inside. At this stage it is an archetypal pattern, unformed in any way we can appreciate. It then clothes itself in the images, emotions, and behavior we have experienced in our life as well as those we have learned of at second-hand through art, entertainment and education.

First the pattern forms. As it emerges it catches our attention, so that we listen, we *focus*. My experience leads me to be believe that perhaps focus is the necessary catalyst for synchronicity to occur. Transitional times take us out of the mundane "robot" existence we normally lead and cause us to focus on our life. Once we notice a synchronicity and open ourselves to the possibility of other synchronicities, we become ever more focused. A good metaphor for the process might be that synchronicity serves as a lens that concentrates the diffuse world of the unconscious until it emerges into consciousness. When a visual lens focuses diffuse light, the light becomes more and more intense. Focused enough, it can actually cause combustion. Similarly with the focus that synchronicities bring into our lives, though here the combustion creates not flames, but *meaning*. (14)

It may be difficult to imagine how archetypes can organize not only our inner world, but outer events as well. Jung's answer is that archetypes are *psychoid;* i.e., both physical and psychical. This is a strange way of viewing things which tends to turn our normal view of reality, even paranormal reality, on its head. For example, think about Dr. Reed's "The Getting to Know You Game." We presented it for simplicity as if there was a speaker or agent and one or more receivers. But we can also view the same situation as if an archetype of relationship is being awakened and because of its psychoid nature, the entire environment, including all the people are acausally connected in a meaningful event. This is most pronounced in the "soul retrieval" version we mentioned earlier, in which a consciously chosen archetypal fairy tale structure is used as the organizational principle. Because this outer format closely matches what is actually going on in the experiment, it is especially powerful for the participants.

Saliency

When we try to understand nature, we should look at the phenomena as if they were messages *to be understood. Except that each message appears to be random until we establish a code to read it. This code takes the form of an abstraction, that is, we choose to ignore certain things as irrelevant and we thus partially select the content of the message by a free choice. These irrelevant signals form the "background noise," which will limit the accuracy of our message.*

J. M. Jauch. (15)

Jung conceived of synchronicity as an explanatory principle to deal with meaningful acausality. Unfortunately, it is this very acausality that causes traditional science to dismiss synchronicity out of hand, no matter how many seeming examples are presented. Classically, science has been based on physical cause-and-effect. Relativity demonstrated the equivalence of matter and energy, which somewhat diluted the picture. Quantum mechanics brought probability into the equation so that, at the quantum level, we could no longer speak of direct cause-and-effect, simply of probabilities of outcomes. More recently still, a new factor--information--has moved into a central position. Mathematician, psychiatrist, and experimental psychologist William Sulis has proposed that naturally occurring complex systems are information driven. Since almost everything in nature of much interest is a complex system, information moves to the forefront and Sulis proposes an alternative to physical or energetic causality, which he terms *saliency*. "The critical issue is not whether information is present, for that will always be the case, but rather whether or not the information which is present is salient for the system in contact with it." (16) In other words, the environment might be filled with information, but information is only useful when its complement is found.

Even random noise can be seen as filled with information for an organism that needs something to complement itself. In other words, saliency is neither in the organism nor in the environment, but only in the coming together of both. Saliency provides a scientifically rigorous alternative to causality. Notice that not only have we moved past the concept of mechanical or energetic causality, we are now dealing with a total pattern which includes both what would formerly have been viewed as the cause and the effect. Both are now part of a single pattern in which the information in one links with the information in the other in order for something new to emerge. What is that link? I would suggest it is "meaning," though Sulis, like any good pure scientist, objects to finding meaning in nature. Commenting further about synchronicity and saliency, however, he comes very close to the position we are taking in this paper when he says that "I like to think of reality like a giant ocean, and synchronicity like the currents. There are many differing currents. Some are local, some are global. One can form endless patterns but some are mere random fluctuations, while others are significant. Not knowing the currents can get one killed. Knowing the currents one can travel far. Not everywhere mind you. And not always in the way planned or desired. It is knowing when to go with the flow, and when to cross the flow." (17)

We can see examples of saliency occurring at many different levels broadly throughout nature, from the sub-atomic level upwards. At the behavioral level, the relatively new science of *ethology* provides us with a wealth of material. Ethology is the scientific study of animal behavior, especially as it occurs in a natural environment.

Innate Animal Behaviors

There was never a king like Solomon
Not since the world began
Yet Solomon talked to a butterfly
As a man would talk to a man.

- Rudyard Kipling. [18]

It seems nonsensical how much resistance science still has to Jung's archetypal hypothesis, since we have ample evidence that the brain itself appears to preserve its evolutionary history within its structure. Every human brain contains an immense number of behaviors that have proved useful for our ancestors in the human and animal world over vast periods of time. Certain situations repeat over and over for every member of a species. For example, frogs have to be very good at recognizing flies or they will go hungry. Humans have to be very good at recognizing human faces or they can't function within any human social structure. So there has to be a great deal of specificity in what is stored in the brain. [19] On the other hand, every creature is in large part born into a world unique to it.

For example, though all creatures are born from a mother and, in a majority of species, are raised by the mother, mothers come in a great variety of different packages. Nature has to handle both the specificity and the variety. In his *King Solomon's Ring,* Nobel prize winning ethologist Konrad Lorenz explains that "greylag goslings unquestioningly accept the first living being whom they meet as their mother." (20) Lorenz experimented with this "imprinting" behavior and often served as surrogate mother for a variety of little creatures. In the preface, there is a lovely drawing Lorenz did of himself, a friend, and a number of animals. He describes the scene:

> First came a big red dog, looking like an Alaskan husky, but actually a cross between an Alsatian and a Chow, then two men in bathing trunks carrying a canoe, then ten half-grown greylag goslings, walking with all the dignity characteristic of their kind, then a long row of thirteen tiny cheeping mallard ducklings, scurrying in pursuit, forever afraid of being lost and anxiously striving to keep with the larger animals. At the end of the procession marched a queer piebald ugly duckling, looking like nothing on earth, but in reality a hybrid of ruddy sheldrake and Egyptian goose. But for the bathing trunks and the moving picture camera slung across the shoulders of the men, you might have thought you were watching a scene out of the garden of Eden. (21)

The mallards were a triumph for Lorenz, as, for quite a while, he hadn't been able to figure out how to make them see him as mother. Through some detective work, he figured out that it wasn't enough to be the first person they saw at birth; in addition, he "must quack like a mother mallard in order to make the little ducks run after me." That turned out to do the trick. Though he looked about as much like a mother mallard "as Calvin Coolidge looks like Metro Goldwyn Mayer's lion" (as James Thurber so perfectly described the wolf masquerading as Red Riding Hood's grandmother in his *Fables for our Time*), "anything that emits the right quack note will be considered as mother." (22)

Nor are such inherited behaviors limited to newborns. Courting rituals are also instinctive in many species. An adult male jackdaw fell in love with Lorenz and tried all the wiles that normally proved successful with female jackdaws. For example, he kept trying to feed Lorenz delicacies like ground-up worms. Like a true scientist, Lorenz suffered this disgusting diet as long as he could. When he was finally so sick of the taste of worms that he refused to open his mouth, the jackdaw filled his ear with worms, then was disappointed when this proved a less than successful romantic strategy. (23)

A baby's recognition of mother, an adult's repertoire of courting behavior, both innate. Recognition of danger is also often inborn. "Magpies, mallards or robins, prepare at once for flight at their very first sight of a cat, a fox or even a squirrel. They behave in just the same way, whether reared by man or by their own parents." In contrast, jackdaws, who we have seen are born knowing so much about love, have to be taught to recognize danger by their parents. Though they may not be born with a sense of self-preservation, they are, however, born with an innate need to protect their young at all costs. Since jackdaws--including baby jackdaws--are black, "any living being that carries a black thing, dangling or fluttering, becomes the object of furious onslaught." Poor Lorenz discovered this to his distress when he accidentally picked up a baby jackdaw and was instantly attacked by the mother. He dropped the baby, and was left with a wounded and bloody hand. Now forewarned, Lorenz systematically explored just how far this instinctual behavior extended. He found, for example, that he could safely carry his black camera, but "the jackdaws would start their rattling cry as soon as I pulled out the black paper strips of the pack film which fluttered to and fro in the breeze." This happened even though the adult birds knew Lorenz to be their friend and no threat to their children. Instinct simply took over. (24)

Does Synchrony + Saliency = Synchronicity?

Though we have a considerably greater ability to take conscious control of our actions than a jackdaw, a huge amount of our behaviors are already stored away at birth in the psyche, ready to be triggered into action when needed. Key is that these examples and the others that

Lorenz provided of mating behavior and defensive behavior, are inborn predispositions that are triggered by highly specific information cues from the environment. An image of lock and key comes to mind, which brings us back to saliency. Imagine these cognitive invariants as wholly contained behaviors (with accompanying predispositions toward images) which are locked until a highly specific key appears in the environment to open the lock and release the behavior. Note that this is not either physically or energetically causal; information is all that is exchanged. Neither the mother nor child causes the experience of the mother/child relationship to be activated; rather both together form this new whole. If the imprinting has occurred as it should onto a mother gosling or mallard, the other side of the relationship would have also been triggered. In Sulis' words: "Saliency does not depend upon the energy which is exchanged but rather upon the form, texture, and context within which the exchange takes place. Pattern takes precedence over substance." (25)

Jung viewed synchronicity as a subset of acausal events in general, one in which meaning was central, psychological meaning. But saliency allows us to stretch the concept of meaning down to a point where it no longer has to be psychological meaning. Saliency can occur without synchronicity but synchronicity cannot occur without saliency. Sulis and the author both agree that synchronicity in an extended sense pervades reality; that is, there are many more acausally linked events happening at any point in time than causal events. And even causal events are better viewed within the broader view of saliency and multivariance.

Saliency provides a way to approach synchrony, and from synchrony to synchronicity. Imagine a room full of pendulum clocks, initially all at rest. Then, one at a time, start each pendulum moving. If you're careful, at first you may be able to have all of them at different parts of the cycle of their swing. for example, one might be just starting its downward swing, one may have reached the bottom of its swing, ready to move up again, a third might have reached the peak of its swing, ready to move backward once more. If you leave them alone for a while, then come back, you may be surprised to find that now they all swing together in perfect harmony. The movement of each has had an effect on each of the others, Gradually they come to a single rhythm which harmonizes all the movements.

In physical systems, this mutual feedback of *salient* information is termed *entrainment*. It operates in biological systems as well as in physical systems. For example, that's why crickets chirp together rather than at random, why groups of fireflies tend to flash at the same time. There have been experiments that show when women are living together isolated from others, their menstrual cycles come into balance in the same way. Or reconsider the lovely example we gave earlier in our discussion of synchrony, of the little girl who led the entire school yard into her rhythmic movement. We could say that the girl's movement caused each of the other children in turn to match her rhythm, but it's more elegant to think of the rhythm already being there and gradually the whole playground matched the rhythm. The little girl was the first to tap into the rhythm and part of that movement included her moving all around the playground. If the rhythm had been strong enough, it might well have pervaded the playground even if the little girl didn't move throughout the whole playground.

Whether we term it saliency or meaning, the universe is filled with information. Meaning pervades the universe at every level, and we barely tap that source of limitless meaning. That meaning lies behind our personal destinies as much as it defines the movements of stars in the sky. We have only to find the right keys for the locks that open the gateways. And the key is often synchronicity.

REFERENCES

1. Marie-Louise von Franz, *Time: Rhythm and Repose* (New York: Thames and Hudson, 1978), p. 22.

2. This and previous quote are from Edward T. Hall, *Beyond Culture* (Garden City, New York: Anchor Books, 1977), p. 72, 73.

3. Edward T. Hall, *Beyond Culture,* p. 77.

4. Henry Reed, "Intimacy and Psi: Explorations in Psychic Closeness," *Journal of Analytical Psychology 41, Par 1* (1986), p. 81..

5. private communication from Dr. Henry Reed.

6. F. David Peat, Synchronicity: The Bridge Between Matter and Mind *(New York: Bantam, 1987), p. 27.*

7. Ira Progoff, *Jung, Synchronicity, and Human Destiny* (New York: Dell, 1973), p. 132.

8. Victor Mansfield, *Synchronicity, Science and Soul-Making* (Chicago: Open Court, 1995), p. 26.

9. Aniela Jaffé, *From the Life and Work of C.G. Jung,* R. F. C. Hull and Murray Stein, trans. (Am Klosterplatz, Einsiedeln: Switzerland: Daimon Verlag, 1989), p. 20.

10. C.G. Jung, "Approaching the Unconscious" in C. G. Jung, editor, *Man and His Symbols* (New York: Anchor Books, Doubleday, 1964), p. 55.

11. C. G. Jung, *Memories, Dreams, Reflections,* revised edition (New York: Pantheon Books, 1973), pp. 155-6.

12. Aniela Jaffé, *Apparitions and Precognition* (New Hyde Park, New York: University Books, 1963), p. 191.

13. Aniela Jaffé, *Apparitions and Precognition* (New Hyde Park, New York: University Books, 1963), p. 192.

14. This idea that focus creates meaning is, by the way, basically the same theme that Colin Wilson explores throughout most of this books, though he doesn't address synchronicity per se.

15. J. M. Jauch, quotation in Sarah Voss, What Number Is God?: Metaphors, Metaphysics, Metamathematics, and the Nature of Things *(New York: SUNY Press, 1995), p. 103.*

16. William F. Sulis, unpublished paper for UNESCO conference, 1999.

17. William. F. Sulis, private email correspondence of 5/11/99.

18. quoted in the preface to Konrad Lorenz, *King Solomon's Ring* (New York: Time Incorporated, 1952), p. xxi.

19. James A. Anderson and Edward Rosenfeld, eds., *Neurocomputing: Foundations of Research* (Cambridge: MIT Press, 1988), p. 2.

20. Konrad Lorenz, *King Solomon's Ring,* p.47.

21. Konrad Lorenz, *King Solomon's Ring,* pp. xxiv-xxv.

22. Konrad Lorenz, *King Solomon's Ring,* p. 48.

23. Konrad Lorenz, *King Solomon's Ring,* pp. 153-4.

24. Konrad Lorenz, *King Solomon's Ring,* pp. 157-9.

25. William F. Sulis, unpublished paper for UNESCO conference, 1999.

A UNITARY WORLD

THE BRAIN AND ITS PLACE IN JUNG'S PSYCHOID REALITY

The common background of microphysics and depth-psychology is as much physical as psychic and therefore neither, but rather a third thing, a neutral nature which can at most be grasped in hints since its essence is transcendental. The background of our empirical world thus appears to be in face a unus mundus. This is at least a probably hypothesis which satisfies the basic tenet of scientific theory: "Explanatory principles are not to be multiplied beyond the necessary" (Jung, CW14: 768-9).

No aspect of C. G. Jung's psychological model is more controversial and misunderstood than his concept of the *archetypes of the collective unconscious;* i.e., inherited predispositions which underlie instinctual behavior and/or the images of such behaviors which appear in dreams. He argued that *archetypes* are contained in all human beings (and by extension in all animals containing a sufficiently complex neural structure). As his work progressed, he came to believe in a *unus mundus* (unitary world), which underlay both *psyche* and body. He also often referred to this unitary world as a model of *psychoid* reality; i.e., the reality we all live in, which we experience alternately as psyche or matter, but which Jung argued was both and neither.

Jung's self-exploration, work with patients, and study of mythology all combined to make him realize that there were two progressively larger strata beneath consciousness: (1) the personal unconscious (where personal memories are stored that we have either repressed or simply never brought into consciousness); and (2) the collective unconscious (where the entire history of the evolution of consciousness appears to be stored.) In actuality, the collective unconscious is nothing mystical. As we will see, our bodies themselves are a virtual storehouse of the entire history of life leading up to present day humanity. Every living creature at birth already has a wealth of behavioral possibilities stored in the brain and body. If not, they would never survive. As the level of complexity of animals rises, the complexity and subtlety of the inherited behaviors (or possibilities of behaviors) grows. By the time when dreams came into existence, (a minimum of 65 million years ago), the ability to access information symbolically also became stored, so that now we had access to not only inherited behaviors but inherited symbolic behaviors.

This paper will present several disparate contemporary models of the brain, in order to show how these well they support Jung's own model. We will be considering the following:

- Paul Maclean's Triune Model;
- Konrad Lorenz's discoveries of innate animal behaviors;
- the Computer Model of the brain so loved by cognitive psychology;
- Gerald Edelman's theory of Neural Darwinism;
- Neural Networks; and
- Karl Pribram's model of a Holographic Brain within a Holographic World.

The Triune Brain

Unless one wished to return to a complete psychophysical dualism, it was best to consider external states as the expression of internal states, which could, moreover, exist independently of this expression (Jeannerod, 1985, pp. 84-5).

The first thing we need to appreciate about the brain is that it is really made up of a series of individual brains, each of which evolved at different points in time. Neurophysiologist Paul MacLean's research shows that there are three distinct brains which combine within what we term the brain. The most ancient, the *reptile brain*, is located at the top of the brain stem which leads into the spinal cord. Wrapped around it is the *mammal brain*, more properly the limbic system. And wrapped around it is the most recent brain, the neocortex, that almost infinitely wrinkled surface which we normally think of as the *human brain*. Though all three brains necessarily communicate to some extent, in large part they take care of their own business without interference from each other. And that causes some interesting complexities of human behavior.

The *reptile brain*, for example, handles issues of aggression, territoriality, social hierarchies, and ritual. Thus when we get "territorial" over "our" toys, "our" boy friend or girl friend, "our" status, "our" scientific discovery, the emotional response wouldn't be out of place in a dog or a cat or a bird or a fish or even a dinosaur. All react from essentially the same reptile brain, which dates back a quarter of a billion years.

The *mammal brain* "governs social awareness and relationships--belonging, caring, empathy, compassion and group preservation" (*Brain/Mind Bulletin*, 1982, p. 4). So the emotional behaviors that we consider to represent humanity at its best, are hardly unique to human beings. They appeared a hundred and fifty million years ago, long before human beings appeared on the scene. Given their longer histories, we would do well to look to other mammals for examples of how we could improve our own behavior in these areas. Wolves, for example, are superb exemplars for caring, compassionate parenting. When Richard Adams wrote *Watership Down* (Adams, 1972), I think many of us were surprised how easy it was to relate to rabbits. Now it's true that they were rather anthropomorphized rabbits, but there was still a "rabbitness" to them that was both fascinatingly different, yet somehow also recognizably close to human feeling.

Finally at the top of the evolutionary ladder, the neocortex appears: the *human brain*. Though it first emerged in the higher mammals "several tens of millions of years ago . . . its development accelerated greatly a few million years ago when humans emerged" (Sagan, 1977, p. 58). Many neuro-scientists believe that a great deal of this brain evolved out of the need to increase visual acuity. The cognitive abilities we treasure so highly appeared as an offshoot of that new visual proficiency. (Though as we will see later in this paper, perhaps smell precedes sight in its claim on the increased complexity of the brain.)

The fact that each of these three brains is largely independent of the others, helps explain much of our most paradoxical behaviors, in which we seem to be at war within ourselves. In his *Maps of the Mind*, Charles Hampden-Turner gives this ironic summary of what the world would be like if MacLean were right (and he is):

> Tradition in this culture might locate precise thoughts in the mind, but vague emotions in the heart, breast, bowels, blood, nerves or viscera (which are indeed controlled by the limbic or mammalian brain.) . . . Such a culture might be split between cerebral conceptions of science and the expressive arts, the two barely on speaking terms (Hampden-Turner, 1981, p. 82).

Novelist and Renaissance man C. P. Snow popularized this last split between the scientific and artistic worlds with his famed term "the two cultures" (Snow, 1959). His entire work, especially his famed series of eleven novels, *Strangers and Brothers,* can be seen in large part as an accurate representation of the interaction between these two views of reality over the course of the twentieth century. Though Snow's own view of the possibility of reconciling these inherent conflicts was largely pessimistic, he saw, however, hope in our ability to get beyond individual needs and desires.

> But this isn't all. One looks outside oneself to other lives, to which one is bound by love, affection, loyalty, obligation: each of those lives has the same irremediable components as one's own; but there are also components that one can help, or that can give one help. It is in this tiny extension of the personality, it is in this seizing on the possibilities of hope, that we

become more fully human (Snow, 1963, p. 62). [Author's note: or is it more fully animal?]

Though these three brains may be in conflict, they also have necessarily learned to cooperate in order to survive and flourish. The coordination between the reptile and mammal brains is, of course, better than their coordination with the neocortex, simply because they have had so much more time to learn to co-exist. Interestingly, MacLean sees our best hope for unifying the three brains in the act of creativity.

Konrad Lorenz and the Mother Archetype

. . . there is good reason for supposing that the archetypes are the unconscious images of the instincts themselves, in other words, that they are patterns of instinctual behaviors . . . The hypothesis of the collective unconscious is, therefore, no more daring than to assume there are instincts . . . The question is simply this: are there or are there not unconscious universal forms of this kind? If they exist, then there is a region of the psyche which one can call the collective unconscious (Jung, CW9i*:91f).*

As we have seen in the discussion of Paul Maclean's concept of the triune brain, our brains contain our evolutionary history within their very structure. And that ancient structure still controls much of the life we think that we live so consciously. In order to do so, those structures must be highly organized, so that they can still be accessed as needed. If our evolutionary past is stored within us, there are only two ways they can appear in our lives:

(1) *through behavioral actions in the outer world* - that is what we normally term instinct; and

(2) *through images in our inner world* - which Jung initially termed *primordial images* and later *archetypes* (from the Greek for *prime imprinter*).

Jung gradually came to consider an archetype to be a formless pattern which underlay both instinctual behaviors and primordial images. The late distinguished ethologist Konrad Lorenz won the Nobel prize for his careful study of the way instinctual behavior is triggered in animals. He found that animals (including human men and women, of course) are born with inner predispositions toward certain highly specific behaviors. A particular instinctual behavior may lie quiescent in the animal for years, until the time arrives when it is needed. When that time arrives, this inborn, collective behavior is triggered by specific outer stimuli. Lorenz termed this process "imprinting." (**Remember that the word "archetype" derives from the Greek for "prime imprinter"**).

Now, in effect, Lorenz was resurrecting the scientifically unfashionable theory of instincts, but he provided a new piece to the puzzle: by careful observation of how imprinting occurred, he was able to provide the details of how such instinctual behaviors actually operate. For example, while studying the behavior of geese, Lorenz was present when a gosling was hatched. Because Lorenz was the first thing the baby goose saw on waking into life, it imprinted the mother archetype onto Lorenz; i.e., the baby goose decided that Lorenz was its mother (Lorenz, 1952). Now Lorenz didn't look anything like a goose. Nor did he talk like a goose, act like a goose, etc. Therefore, the mother archetype certainly couldn't be stored inside the goose as a picture of what a mother goose should look like. The archetype had to be flexible enough to adapt to a personal experience of mother as different from a normal mother goose as Konrad Lorenz happens to be. That's what Jung meant by insisting that archetypes were formless.

The example given is hardly a singular one. In a previous article (*Synchronicity in a New Light,* Psychological Perspectives #43), I told of a pet jackdaw who fell in love with Lorenz and tried to court him by feeding him ground-up worms, just as if Lorenz were a female jackdaw. I also told there of inherited recognition of danger in several species. In his classic book *Archetypes,* Anthony Stevens gave an example of an innate recognition of danger. Finches flourished on the Galapagos islands because

> . . . the islands possessed no falcons or large birds of prey. For hundreds of thousands of years these finches

> had never had to cringe or demonstrate alarm as a predator flew overhead because they had never seen one. Nevertheless, when . . . thirty specimens, drawn from four different species, arrived in California, . . . they all emitted alarm calls and cringed whenever a predatory bird, such as a raven or a red-tailed hawk, came in sight (Stevens, 1983, p. 48).

What other explanation can there be for such behavior than that the finches possessed an archetype of danger specific enough to be triggered by large birds of prey?

The Digital Computer Model of the Brain/Mind

Man seeks to form for himself, in whatever manner is suitable for him, a simplified and lucid image of our world, and so to overcome the world of experience by striving to replace it to some extent by this image.

- Albert Einstein (Holton, 1973, pp. 376-7).

Throughout history, thinkers have turned to cutting-edge science and technology for new metaphors for thought. This is enormously productive for generating new views of reality, but such metaphors also need to be viewed with some skepticism. In the late seventeenth century, for example, when Descartes looked for a model of the brain, he turned to hydraulics. Though, to us, this seems an eccentric choice, hydraulics was the most advanced technology of the time, and thus seemed a perfectly reasonable choice to Descartes.

In his model, the pineal gland, which lies behind the middle of the forehead, was "the seat of imagination and common sense." It received information from our senses, then formed an image. So far, if we substituted the brain for the pineal gland, it would sound much like the normal, though outmoded, view of perception still taught in school. But then comes the hydraulics: the pineal gland actually leans toward the "side bearing the image"--which sounds like a Rube Goldberg device--that then opened or closed certain tubes.

> Sensory stimulation produced a flux of the animal spirts contained in the heart and arteries. The heart then pushed the spirits into the cerebral cavities, much as the pumps of an organ push air into its pipes. . . . After death the brain collapsed and fluid could no longer circulate (Jeannerod, 1985, p. 2).

The most prevalent current cognitive model of the brain/mind views the brain as a complex digital computer, and the mind as nothing more than the programs it runs, which are stored within the structure of the brain. Because of the ubiquity of computers within the fabric of modern society, this model seems totally reasonable to many, but times change and the computer model may someday seem as outdated as Descartes' hydraulic model.

With this disclaimer in mind, let's look at the computer as a metaphor for the brain/mind. The same computer can run many different programs, just as a human can perform many different behaviors. Both the computer and the brain store their programs in some sort of long-term memory until they are needed. In addition to the bread-and-butter programs, the computer needs a special program, normally called an operating system (O/S), which operates at a higher level than any of the other programs. An O/S is like a foreman in a factory who keeps things running smoothly. The O/S knows which programs are running in the computer, which are waiting to run, and which have already run. However, the O/S doesn't decide which programs need to be run, just as the foreman doesn't decide what products a factory should make. This is an executive decision; a human operator tells the computer which programs need to be run in what order of importance. The O/S then schedules the programs, locates them in its long-term memory, runs them when it has the time and resources to do so, prints the results and stores the programs away again for later use.

Note that there are at least three levels of operation at work here:

(1) the executive level which decides which programs should be run;
(2) a foreman level which keeps things running smoothly; and
(3) a worker level which does the actual work we associate with the computer.

By analogy, driving a car requires an executive decision on one level of the psyche, the organization and supervision of the necessary behaviors on a second level, and the actual performance of the behaviors on a third level. It is important to realize that only the executive level necessarily involves consciousness. The foreman and worker level can proceed famously without conscious intervention. This latter is an important concept that we can learn from examining this model, even if the model itself proves inadequate.

Just to mention a few diverse examples of the "programs" stored in our brains, we might have stored a program that tells us how to play tennis, another program that enables us to operate a computer much as I am doing now as I write this book. Of course, those high-level programs would in turn be composed of many increasingly smaller programs that would range down to the level of directing the appropriate parts of our body to move. All of us have a series of highly complex programs to draw on in social settings. These programs may or may not have anything to do with consciousness. For example, another program might drive our car for us, even if our conscious attention is elsewhere. The wide variety of programs available to a normal person is almost uncountable.

Though the situation is not as clear as with a computer, we also appear to have a higher-level "foreman" function similar to the operating system of a computer, something which keeps track of the total system, loads and runs programs as necessary, allocates resources where needed, etc. Now already various theorists split at this point, with some arguing against the need for any such central program; it is, however, convenient for our illustration of the digital computer model. Again, consciousness doesn't appear to be involved in this centralized program, any more than it is in the running of any other program. This is not to deny that consciousness can enter the scene and take control of a previously unconscious program; it's just to assert that the human psyche is able to operate quite well even in the limited role of a computer, totally devoid of consciousness.

Computer programs are highly organized groups of abstract symbols, specific to the computer within which they are intended to operate. They are stored in some form of relatively permanent memory accessible by the computer, either by being permanently attached to the computer, or by being able to be read into the computer when necessary. The programs of the human psyche must be to some extent similar. The storage might be something obvious, like a record of synaptic changes in the brain, or less obvious, like a pattern of musculature in the body.

The operating system of the human psyche, like the operating system of a computer, necessarily operates at a higher level than the application programs of the psyche. Earlier, I used the analogy of "workers" for the application programs and "foreman" for the operating system, with the "executive" on top making the decisions that the "foreman" organizes and the "workers" carry out. In the psyche, consciousness seemingly forms the highest level of that analogy: the decision maker. If our analogy between computer and human mind can be extended this far, the operating system must also be a program, albeit a highly complex program. In a computer, the most significant parts of the operating system are usually stored in part in a permanent, extremely compact form on one or more computer chips. This makes this part of the operating system incredibly fast at performing necessary repetitive tasks. The remainder of the operating system is stored as software, much like any other program, except that its function is to control the entire computer.

The human equivalent to the part of the operating system stored on permanent computer chips might be the entire structure of the human body, with a special emphasis on the DNA structure in the genes, and the nervous system culminating in the human brain. But the entire body structure contributes to the control of itself in ways much more complex than any existing computer. However, the analogy is still close enough for our purposes so we will leave it there for now. We will see its limitations as we learn a little more about the brain and its operation.

Natural Selection

The brain is a selective system more akin in its working to evolution than to computation or information processing (Edelman, 1987, p. 25).

In our discussion of MacLean's triune model of the brain, we saw that our brain is actually a repository of hundreds of millions of years of evolutionary experience. The example of the gosling who thought Konrad Lorenz was his mother showed how behaviors stored in the brain actually affect an animal's life. Stored behavioral patterns kick in at virtually every important stage of life, and similar behaviors are, of course, also innate in humans, though we have more conscious control over exercising them.

Charles Darwin's theory of evolution by natural selection provides the most commonly accepted explanation for how such behaviors can be innate. Take

Stevens' example of inherited recognition of danger. Darwin's theory would argue that the finches who were quickest to recognize enemies were more likely to survive and have children. If their children recognized such enemies at birth, they would be more likely to survive. Those finch, who were, by nature, slower to recognize potential threats, would have fewer children survive. So the next generation would have more finches who were quick to recognize potential enemies, and so forth. Though there are limitations to Darwin's theory which are being explored now in science, we don't need to deal with those for our purposes here.

As Darwin's theory became almost universally accepted by science, it was natural for late nineteenth century theoreticians of the brain to recognize that "the complexity of the behavior of an animal reflects the complexity of its nervous system and thus that evolutionary changes in anatomy can give rise to new behavior patterns" (Edelman, 1987, p. 10). Only recently though has this recognition led to a scientifically sophisticated model of the brain. Nobel prize winner Gerald M. Edelman adds a major twist to this understanding with his theory of Neural Darwinism, which goes a long way toward explaining the remarkable ability of the human brain to adapt to a variety of circumstances.

In brief, Edelman looks at the growth and development of an individual brain as a process of natural selection. Because of the evolutionary history of the human brain, it already contains incredible numbers of groups of interconnected neurons. A rough estimate is one *hundred billion neurons,* connected into groups, with each such neuron group including anywhere from *50 to 10,000 neurons* connected in highly complex ways. Our genes determine the initial connections of neurons into neuron groups. During the gestation period, the growth and development of the brain of the fetus is accompanied by a *selection* of perhaps a million such neuron groups. He calls this the *primary repertoire*; in other words, the possibilities which are wired-in at birth. But such hard-wired behavior is hardly sufficient to deal with the variety of the world. As Edelman argues:

> An individual animal endowed with a richly structured brain must also adapt without instruction to a complex environment to form perceptual categories or an internal taxonomy governing its further responses to the world (Edelman, 1987, pp. 8-9).

Again remember Lorenz' example of how the goslings decided Lorenz was "mother," simply because he was the first thing they saw on waking into life. This is clearly a strategy for adapting to the variety of situations baby geese might encounter at birth, and is built-in genetically.

But as soon as these innate behaviors have kicked in, experience starts modifying the brain. For example, at birth both of a human baby's eyes are connected to all the neurons in the brain's visual cortex. But experience forces each eye to select neural connections for itself, effectively taking them away from the other eye. Since we use both eyes equally, eventually each has about half the pathways, with the resulting neuron groups looking nothing like what they were at birth. If for some reason, one eye was covered continuously during that developmental stage, the other eye would have all the neural pathways. That would mean that the eye that had been covered could still see the world, but the information would never get to the brain.

> In the broad view across taxa, behavior is remarkably diverse and its relation to neural structure appears to be almost capricious. To wiggle the tail of a worm may take a network of thousands of neurons but to flick the tail of a fish only one (Edelman, 1987, p. 23).

Why is this? Shouldn't evolution gradually make the brain's processes more and more efficient over time? In fact, most digital computer models of the brain view the programs it stores as logical algorithms, i.e., "a step-by-step problem-solving procedure, especially an established, recursive computational procedure for solving a problem in a finite number of steps" (*American Heritage Talking Dictionary,* 1997). Philosopher of science Larry R. Vandervert provides the most extreme view of this model with his theory of "neurological positivism." He views evolution as refining the algorithms of the brain to ever more perfect functionality, so that the brain, mind and world form a unity in which it is possible to transform any one into the other through pre-determined transformational rules.

This is a lovely model which may be largely true except for its assumption that evolution keeps honing the algorithms to every-increasing perfection. The brain doesn't form its programs this way, since in any generation, animals who have to come up with new behaviors to fit new situations draw on the existing structures of the brain, selecting whatever works, then modifying it as is needed.

> . . . the brain is not constructed to think abstractly -- it is constructed to ensure survival in the world. It has many of the characteristics of a good engineering solution applied to mental operation: do as good a job as you can, cheaply, and with what you can obtain easily. If this means using ad hoc solutions, with less generality than one might like, so be it. We are living in a particular world, and we are built to work in it and with it (Anderson and Rosenfeld, 1988, p. 1).

Another short quote from Edelman brings this all together: "A central assumption of the theory is that perceptual categorization must both precede and accompany learning" (Edelman, 1987, p. 7). We have already built-in many more brain structures than we will ever use. During gestation, we select a healthy-sized group of those structures to draw on in life. After birth we start connecting those together *and modifying them* as we adapt to our environment. The brain grows large and more complex; by the time we reach maturity, the human brain is four times bigger than it was at birth and "no two individual animals are likely to have identical connectivity in corresponding brain regions" (Edelman, 1987, p. 5). Each little gosling is able to follow Lorenz, behaving for all the world knows in identical fashion. Yet each is unique.

Now from the above, we can already see another major problem with the digital computer model of the brain. In digital computers, programs, once written, remain unchanged. Perhaps there is some degradation in the storage and retrieval process, but that invariably makes the program no longer run correctly; it can't in any way be viewed as analogous to mutations. In nature, we find in contrast that in many cases a behavior that fits one circumstance can adapt itself to a new circumstance. If the brain is a storehouse of programs, some stored permanently across generations, others only during the course of a person's life, those programs must be something different than the programs stored in a digital computer. Much more like the neuron groups Edelman presents.

Long before we knew much about the actual structure of the brain, psychologist William James already realized that the brain exists as part of the world, not as a compilation of logical, immutable algorithms.

> *Mental facts cannot properly be studied apart from the physical environment of which they take cognizance* . . . our inner faculties are *adapted* in advance to the features of the world in which we dwell. . . . Mind and world in short have evolved together, and in consequence are something of a mutual fit (Anderson and Rosenfeld, 1988, p. 1).

That recognition of the joint evolution of mind and world is as true today as when James wrote it a century ago.

Neural Networks

In the neural network model of the mind, thinking is not following a set of rules but a product of the complex interactions of huge numbers of neurons (Allman, 1989, p. 22).

In the computer model of the brain we presented earlier, actions were accomplished hierarchically: an executive decision (by consciousness), was supervised by a foreman level, who in turn had workers accomplish the tasks. The neurological equivalent of the workers are "hard-wired" connections between, for example, different receptors in our eyes and neurons in the brain. Groups of neurons are specialized in order to solve specific tasks; e.g., detecting edges, separating various curves, making color discriminations, and so forth. These hard-wired connections are essentially specialized workers who are called into action when we consciously decide to focus our attention somewhere. They are the parts of the brain most like digital computer programs.

Most of these hard-wired connections are directly coded by DNA sequences in our genes. There are living organisms simple enough that every single neural connection is described genetically. But for most animals, and certainly for human beings, our genes hardly begin the task of making such connections. For example, we have already said that at birth both of a baby's eyes are connected to all of the neurons in the visual cortex of the brain. Then experience intensifies some connections and eliminates others until each eye has about half the connections. This is much more efficient than having to describe all those connections genetically. So we end up with specialized workers in the brain, but they didn't have to be fully described genetically. This method of "writing programs" is similar to how simple programs often referred to as "macros" are created within word-processing, spreadsheet or data base programs. Basically, you notify the computer to begin recording a macro, then you perform a series of tasks, then turn off the recording when you're done. The resulting macro program is stored and available for later use.

But much more of the brain's solutions to problems don't involve such hard-wiring at all. Nor do they involve the hierarchical, logical solutions of the digital computer model. Instead "best-fit" solutions are arrived at in a way that seems like heresy to those who believe in a strictly cognitive model of the brain. "Computers are typically given a list of instructions to follow. A neural network, on the other hand, is "taught" through a series of examples" (Allman, 1989, p. 12). This new way of viewing the brain has been termed the *neural network* model.

A good metaphor for how this model works is a small town meeting. Imagine that everyone in the town has gathered in the town hall to discuss some problem that concerns everyone to a greater or lesser extent. Let's say that they are considering changing the zoning laws so that some land previously zoned for residence only is now going to be opened up for commercial interests. Since this is a small town, everyone in the room has some connection to everyone else, but the strength of those connections may vary considerably. For example, some people may be relatives, others friends, others acquaintances, still others business colleagues. At the start of the session, some people will probably already have definite feelings one way or the other about the issue. For example, the proposition will undoubtedly have been presented by businessmen who want to make use of this land. They will already have made connections with others to try and win them over to their point-of-view. In contrast, those with homes near the area under discussion may be strongly opposed to having it opened up for commercial use. They will probably have already talked this over with some friends as well.

So, as the meeting begins, there are already some people with strong feelings for and against the proposition. But it's likely that most people won't yet have formed any opinion. When the meeting begins, the two opposing sides present their cases. As they do, those who were initially indifferent to the issue begin to lean one way or the other. They may do this on the basis of the issues or simply on the basis of their personal or business connections with someone on either side of the issue. Remember that the strength of the connections between people will vary considerably. As the discussion continues, there will be rising and ebbing tides as one side or the other gains temporary ascendence. Gradually the discussion will begin to die down as everyone eventually comes to a decision. A consensus will emerge and the new zoning will either be accepted or turned down.

When everyone leaves the meeting, not only is the issue solved, but the strength of their connections with each other may have changed during the session, not only on this issue but in general. Someone may realize that they really should spend more time with some person who impressed them. Or they may have formed an antipathy to another person simply on the basis of what they said or how they behaved in the meeting. No one could have predicted in advance exactly who would end up for and against the proposal and how strongly they would feel about it. The final outcome is a unique solution to the original problem, one that would be impossible to logically dissect.

This "town meeting" model is a close approximation to how the brain solves many problems. Just imagine that the neurons in the brain are the townspeople and the strength of the connections between various neurons varies just as the townspeople vary in their feelings of attachment to each other. At any point in time, when some new solution needs to be created by the brain, the neurons are in various stages of activation, just as the townspeople were at the start of the meeting. As impulses flow between the various connections, some neurons turn on and some turn off, depending on the strength of the signal received and other particulars we can ignore in this discussion. Eventually, a new stability arises which leads to a resolution of the original issue, whether it was pattern recognition or a need for action.

In 1982, John Hopfield, a physicist at Cal Tech, proved mathematically that a network of simplified neurons acting in this way, can process information and solve problems (Hopfield, 1982). Logic wasn't needed. Hierarchies weren't needed. The brain can make use of the neuron groups it already has present in order to form new connections and arrive at a generalized solution.

In order to model how this actually works in practice, neuroscientist Gary Lynch collaborated with computer scientist Richard Granger in developing a computer model of a 500 neuron network to see if it could learn to discriminate between different smells. They had two different smell groups: "cheese" and "flower," with variations of each. At first the neural net came up with a unique pattern for each smell, but eventually, after it was exposed to the individual odors more times, the neural net produced one pattern for the cheeses and another for the flowers. Without any instruction or any logic, it was able to generalize from the specific examples to the group to which they belonged. If they exposed it to any of the "cheese" smells, for example, it would always identify "cheese."

But something even more startling happened: as they continued to give it more sniffs of each particular cheese, at some point, the general pattern disappeared and the neural net then produced specific patterns for the various cheeses, within the general pattern. Now the network could not only discriminate "cheeses" from "flowers," but also different varieties of "cheeses." Granger said that:

> We're thrilled with it. With the first sniff, it recognizes the overall pattern and says, "it's a cheese." With the next sniffs, it distinguishes the pattern and says, "It's Jarlsberg" (Allman, 1989, p. 76).

This model which discriminates different smells is a perfect example of a neural net, as the neuron groups formed are essentially random and unpredictable in advance. If the same model were wiped clean of its memory, then trained again, it would again learn to discriminate the smells, but it would do so with a totally different set of connections in the network. Lynch says "Smell isn't spatial or temporal. It doesn't exist in a dimensional world. It's like pure thought" (Allman, 1989, p. 77). We will return to that idea later.

This is especially interesting because mammals were the first animals to develop a keen sense of smell. Developing a keen sense of smell may have been what made first the mammalian brain, then later the primate brain (the cortex), grow in size. Lynch theorizes that when the dinosaurs disappeared, the mammals needed better vision as well as better smell. That produced a different type of neural connection. For example, the brain deals with vision by a combination of both the digital computer solution and the neural net solution. Some areas of vision work like directly wired algorithmic problems solvers, with specific neurons for specific tasks. Other parts work like smell, with no particular wiring necessary. And, in fact, we can train computer versions of neural nets to perform complex visual tasks, such as detecting varieties of curves, much better than the same task can be done simply by direct connections of particular neurons to particular parts of the brain (Allman, 1989, p. 76-7).

Of course, for neural networks to be more than just a model, it is necessary to prove that the brain actually can and does modify itself. It appears that action is the critical element in changing the brain's structure. This was originally recognized by psychologist/philosopher Williams James, who in this area as in so many others, was prescient. James said that "*no mental modification ever occurs which is not accompanied or followed by a bodily change*. . . . Our psychology must therefore take account not only of the conditions antecedent to mental states, but of their resultant consequences as well" (Allman, 1989, pp. 76-7).

More recently, R. Held proposed that every body movement leaves a trace in memory. When the same movement is executed again, it combines with the original trace and the combination is saved in memory. When they are slightly different, the movement program would be modified to take this difference into account. In the words of French neurophysiologist Marc Jeannerod, "action is thus the means of verifying whether a hypothesis conforms to reality (Jeannerod, 1985). p. 132).

From 1959-1974, Held conducted a long series of experiments to test this. When our senses are systematically distorted, by a lens that inverts our vision, for example, we gradually adjust to this until we see perfectly normally again. But this only happens if we are able to move and test *our* inner view of reality (Jeannerod, 1985, p. 133-7). Of course the action can be internal as well as external.

Let's call these neural net solutions "natural programs" to distinguish them from "algorithmic programs" such as the digital computer model of the brain requires. Natural programs have practical advantages over algorithmic programs and nature always likes to improve its odds of success. Because natural programs are stored in an overall pattern, the more times the pattern is accessed from various input situations, the stronger it becomes. Because it is a pattern spread across a wide number of neurons, even if a substantial portion of the neurons are damaged or even destroyed, the pattern can usually still be reproduced from those that remain. If the newly reproduced pattern is less than perfect, it will get better again as it is reused.

Before we leave this section, it is important to emphasize that the neural net solutions of the brain take place between the receptors and the neocortex, the *human brain*. The connections to, from and largely within the mammalian and reptile brains are directly wired, inherited, beyond change due to experience.

Karl Pribram's Holographic World

Thirty spokes join together at one hub,
But it is the hole that makes it operable.
Clay is moulded into a pot,
But it is the emptiness inside that makes it useful.
Doors and windows are cut to make a room,
It is the empty spaces that we use.
Therefore, existence is what we have,
But non-existence is what we use.

Lao Tzu (Mabry, 1995, p. 13).

The world is filled with "things" which capture our attention, but reality itself is composed of emptiness, of hidden structure. It wasn't until physicists were able to descend into the atom in the twentieth century that Western science realized how profoundly "empty" reality actually is. As Lao Tzu already realized over 2,500 years ago, reality has a structure that isn't composed of the things of the world, but of the spaces left between those things. When everything is related to everything else, it is to the spaces between that we need to look.

Cyclic change occurs everywhere against that static background. We see it most notably in the processions of the seasons. French mathematician Joseph Fourier (1768-1830) was actually able to prove that all mathematical functions, no matter how complex (with the exception of some discontinuous examples that need not concern us here), can be represented by the sum of a series of periodic (i.e., cyclic or recurring) functions of different frequencies and amplitudes. These translations of complex mathematical functions into periodic functions are accordingly called *Fourier Transforms*. An example most are familiar with are the variety of brain-waves, which are traditionally broken down into *delta waves* (1/2 to 3-1/2 cycles/sec), *theta waves* (4-7 cycles/sec), *alpha waves* (8-13 cycles/sec), and *beta waves* (14-30 cycles/sec). If you've ever seen an EEG printed, you'll know that the patterns vary widely in height and width. Any person's individual EEG pattern over any substantial period of time is so complex that it will likely never be repeated by anyone in the history of the world. Yet any such pattern can be reproduced by a sum of highly regular, cyclic patterns which we chose to break into groups we called delta, theta, alpha, and beta.

It was the realization that the brain has to be able to process wave forms that led Karl Pribram to his theory of the holographic brain operating within a holographic universe. As you'll recall from our discussion of the brain, memory appears to be largely stored diffusely over the entire surface of the cortex (with more functionally centralized storage in the more ancient parts of the brain). This distributed storage is why computer programs based on the neural net model of the brain appear to learn in similar fashion to the way higher animals learn. What we didn't say then was that the mathematics that underlies this method of storage is based on Fourier Transforms.

It seems natural that the brain should have this capability when we realize that much of the information we take in from the world is in wave form: sound waves, light waves. Even the particles of matter we inhale when eat something or smell something can, at their atomic level, be considered wave as much as particle. Waves have no definition in time or space: a wave is defined simply by its amplitude and its frequency. Once begun, a wave simply continues waving endlessly. Paradoxically, even though our senses process input from the world in the form of waves, in our minds we perceive the world as made up of objects existing in time and space. Thus the brain has to have a mechanism which *transforms* (i.e.

Fourier Transforms) information received in the form of waves into a form we can deal with.

In 1947, drawing on the mathematics of Fourier Transforms, physicist Dennis Gabor proved mathematically that holographic photography was possible. By the early 1960's, with the development of laser beams, holograms became physical realities. A laser beam is a coherent light source; in other words, it's made up of waves with identical amplitudes and frequencies moving along together. To actually create a hologram, you use a prism to split a laser beam into two identical beams, then bounce each off mirrors tilted at 45 degrees, so that they reflect the two beams back to form a single beam again. If done carefully, the recombined light beam is identical to the original beam; that is, the peaks and valleys of the two beams line up exactly.

Now replace one of the mirrors with some object. The light will still be reflected off the object and recombined with the other beam, but instead of being a perfect reflection, the light waves will reflect off the nooks and crannies than make up the structure of the object. Thus, when the two beams recombine, "interference patterns" will be created. That is, the peaks and valleys of the waves won't always coincide, and they will be "out of synch" in complex ways that exactly describe the shape of the object.

Now, what's unique about a hologram is that, if you record that interference pattern on a film, then shine the laser beam back through the film again, it will create a perfect, 3-dimensional image of the object, since the interference pattern is, in this strange way, a perfect portrait of the object.

What is even less obvious is that a hologram thus translates between the physical world of time and space that we think we live in, and the timeless world of the unconscious (and in fact, all reality) that underlies that physical world. An object that exists in time and space is captured in an interference pattern of periodic waves, which have no definition in time or space. Exposed to light, the interference pattern once more generates an object (or at least at this stage of visual holographs, a 3-dimensional portrait of an object) that does exist in time and space. All by way of Fourier Transforms. This capability might, of course, underlie synchronicity. As Karl Pribram comments:

> Wave "numbers" can refer to densities of occurrences with respect to any number of dimensions other than or in addition to time-space. This could mean that physical orders exist in which synchronicity rather than causality operates as a basic principle. . . . This could mean that beyond every appearance of randomness lies hidden an order that awaits discovery (Villoldo and Dychtwald, 1981, p. 102).

In this respect, the universe, composed of an endless stream of waves--one might even call the universe a waving--exists outside of time and space. Since our brains necessarily have the ability to "collapse" those wave forms into perceived particles which exist in time and space, it would be strange indeed if brains did not receive and translate information that can't be expressed in terms of physical cause-and-effect. Everything in reality connects to everything else through the intermingling of wave forms. Relationships are thus largely *acausal*, causality is the exception, not the rule.

The Unus Mundus

Undoubtedly the idea of the unus mundus *is founded on the assumption that the multiplicity of the empirical world rests on an underlying unity, and that not two or more fundamentally different worlds exist side by side or are mingled with one another. Rather, everything divided and different belongs to one and the same world, which is not the world of sense but a postulate whose probability is vouched for by the fact that until now no one has been able to discover a world in which the known law of nature are invalid. That even the psychical world, which is so extraordinarily different from the physical world, does not have its roots outside the one cosmos is evident from the undeniable fact that causal connections exist between the psyche and the body which point to their underlying unitary nature (Jung,* CW14: *767).*

Let's take stock of what we've discovered about the brain and see to what extent it begins to point toward the unitary world Jung proposed underlay all reality, both physical and psychological.

First, we found that we possess not one brain but three, each representing a different stage of evolutionary history and each largely dealing with operations specific to itself. Though we think of ourselves largely as rational beings who make conscious decisions about our lives, a great deal of our behaviors are already stored at birth in the older reptile and mammalian brains. We looked at some examples of how the mother/child relationship, courting behaviors and recognition of danger are built-in for several different species of birds. But quite obviously, such behaviors are also built-in for dogs and cats and monkeys--and humans. Though the development of the neocortex allows us to exercise much more control over those inherited actions than, for example, Lorenz' jackdaw, confused Lorenz with a possible female mate, we would do well to realize just how much of our actions are determined directly by those more primitive brains within us. Then the human brain comes along after the fact and thinks up supposed rational reasons why we were driven by irrational behaviors. This structure is exactly what is needed to support Jung's ideas of a collective unconscious which already possesses vast knowledge acquired over millennia.

We then saw how evolution operates within the structure of those three brains. Each brain, especially the two oldest, can be regarded as a repository of solutions to problems once presented first to species that preceded humans, then later adapted by humans. We've seen that the brain's structure tends to be composed of "good enough" solutions to problems. Where a species needs some special ability specific to itself , such as a frog's need to quickly spot moving bugs, or a human being's need to recognize a wide variety of faces, a new brain structure forms gradually due to evolutionary pressure. But otherwise, if something worked for a lizard that later evolved into a bird, there is no need for the structure to change. If something specific in the bird's environment requires a change in its behavior, the change is likely to be a modification of the original solution rather than something radically new, developed specifically for birds.

Further, there is no evolutionary need for even out-of-date neural structures to disappear, unless they conflict with necessary structures. Doesn't Jung's concept of archetypal structures begin to seem a little less strange, given how the brain has developed? Let's take an example: I think most of us would accept that falling in love must have some such archetypal structure. After all, it happens in very similar ways for all humans in all cultures. In that respect we aren't much different than the jackdaw who fell in love with Lorenz and tried to feed him worms. Human cultures have a wide variety of ways in which that courtship behavior is expressed, so we know that the specific behaviors are not hard-wired, as they are for the jackdaw. But the similarities of behavior are more striking than the cultural differences, or for that matter, even the species differences.

With the increased development of the visual centers of the neocortex, those "good enough" behavioral structures undoubtedly began to form neural linkages with visual structures to provide images that matched to those behaviors, so that archetypes developed two faces - image and behavior - just as Jung argued that they did.. So the concept of a formless archetype that only takes form when experienced in life, begins to seem like a reasonable way to describe the way the brain appears to be structured.

Within limits, the digital computer model of the brain is a fair start at an approximation to the way these hard-wired archetypal structures are stored and function. Just as a computer can load special purpose programs as needed, the brain can call upon special purpose "programs" when it needs them. Some of these programs are written by evolution and stored in the brain's structure at birth, some are learned in the course of our development. These learned but still directly wired programs are probably best exemplified by the connections between some of the receptors in the eyes and the neurons in the visual centers of the brain.

But we also saw that with the increased development of the neocortex in humans (and the higher primates), a second type of brain structure appeared, which can best be represented by neural nets. Rather than a hard-wired solution, the brain instead gradually comes to a solution which is spread widely over the brain's structure (and here, by brain, we are largely talking of the "human brain," the neocortex). We presented a "town hall" model of how this process might operate.

Even more than the hard-wired solutions created by evolution, these "natural programs" (as we termed them), are "just-so" stories. There is no logical necessity for a particular structure to emerge as a solution to a problem; since the solution is spread widely over the structure of the brain, many other possibilities would do just as well.

The neural net model also offers a possibility for Jung's *unus mundus,* his proposed unitary world, to extend past the storage within a single human being. Clearly this method of solving problems and storing memories over an entire structure does the job or nature would never have developed it. At this point, we don't know exactly how it operates, except that it is global rather than local.

Neurophysiologist Karl Pribram was the first to notice that this ability of the brain to store solutions and memories over its entire structure is similar to a hologram, in which a three-dimensional picture may be stored by interference patterns on film. He believes that there are two storage structures going on simultaneously in the brain, one more localized, defined through connections between neurons, another global through the astonishingly numerous dendritic connections within the brain. What is important is that he thinks that the holographic brain is itself a part of a holographic universe. Just as the brain is able to store and access information over its total structure, the universe is able to store and access information over every part of itself, including each human being. Thus, a holographic brain existing within a holographic universe is an explicit realization of Jung's Unus Mundus. Let's give Pribram this last word on our topic, since what he says is so in tune with Jung:

> It isn't that the world of appearances is wrong; it isn't that there aren't objects out there, at one level of reality. It's that if you penetrate through and look at the universe with a holographic system, you arrive at a different view, a different reality. And that other reality can explain things that have hitherto remained inexplicable scientifically: paranormal phenomena, synchronicities, the apparently meaningful coincidence of events (Pribram, 1979, p. 72).

REFERENCES

Adams, Richard *Adams. Watership Down.* New York: MacMillan, 1972.

Allman, William F. Apprentices of Wonder: Inside the Neural Network Revolution. *New York: Bantam Books, 1989.*

American Heritage Talking Dictionary. New York: The Learning Company, Inc., 1997.

Anderson, James A., and Rosenfeld, Edward. (eds.) *Neurocomputing: Foundations of Research.* Cambridge: MIT Press, 1988.

Brain/Mind Bulletin. "Gray's Theory Incorporates Earlier Evolutionary Model of 'Triune Brain,'" *Brain/Mind Bulletin* (March 29, 1982)

Edelman, Gerald M. *Neural Darwinism.* New York: Basic Books, 1987.

Hampden-Turner, Charles. *Maps of the Mind.* New York: MacMillan, 1981.

Holton, Gerald. *Thematic Origins of Scientific Thought.* Cambridge, Harvard University Press, 1973.

Hopfield, J. J. Neural networks and physical systems with emergent collective computational abilities, *Proceedings of the National Academy of Sciences* 79 (1982), pp. 2554-8.

Jeannerod, Marc. *The Brain Machine: The Development of Neurophysiological Thought.* Cambridge, Massachusetts: Harvard University Press, 1985.

Jung, C. G. *The Collected Works of C. G. Jung, Vol. 14: Mysterium Coniunctionis.* Bollingen Series, Princeton: Princeton University Press, 1963. G. Adler & R. F. Hull, eds.

Lorenz, Konrad. *King Solomon's Ring.* New York: Time Incorporated, 1952.

Mabry, John R. (trans.) *The Little Book of the Tao Te Ching.* Rockport, MD: Element Books, 1995.

Pribram, Karl. Holographic Memory: Karl Pribram interviewed by Daniel Goleman. *Psychology Today,* vol. 12, no. 9, Feb. 1979.

Robertson, Robin. *Beginner's Guide to Jungian Psychology.* York Beach, Maine: Nicolas-Hays, Inc., 1992.

Sagan, Carl. The Dragons of Eden: Speculations of the Evolution of Human Intelligence. *New York: Ballantine Books, 1977.*

Snow, C. P. The Two Cultures and the Scientific Revolution, (1959), in C. P. Snow, *Public Affairs.* New York: Charles Scribner's Sons, 1971, pp. 13-46.

Snow, C. P. The Two Cultures: A Second Look, (1963), in C. P. Snow, *Public Affairs.* New York: Charles Scribner's Sons, 1971.

Stevens, Anthony. *Archetypes: A Natural History of the Self.* New York: Quill, 1983.

Villoldo, Alberto and Dychtwald, Ken (eds.). *Millennium: Glimpses into the 21st Century.* Los Angeles: J. P. Tarcher, Inc., 1981.

STAIRWAY TO HEAVEN

JUNG & NEOPLATONISM

Why in the world should we, living in these difficult late days of the 20th century, care about Neoplatonism? What could we possibly find that was *numinous* in a doctrine which flourished in the 2nd through the 5th centuries and died entirely by the 6th century? And what does Neoplatonism have to do with Jung?

Jung has very little to say about Neoplatonism, especially in comparison with his extensive discussions of Gnosticism and alchemy. Jung saw his work somewhat prefigured in the Gnostics of the 1st and 2nd century, but more in the alchemists of the middle ages. And, though Jung mentions Neoplatonism enough times in the *Collected Works* to make it clear he is familiar with its ideas, nowhere does he discuss it as a prefiguration of his work.

So I can't give a straightforward answer to my own question, at least not just yet. In order to understand the importance of Neoplatonism, first we have to understand what Jung found so important in Gnosticism. And that means that we have to go back to the time in Jung's life when he broke with Freud.

Jung's Struggle with the Unconscious

As you'll recall, this was a very difficult period for Jung. He had looked up to Freud as a father figure who could provide answers about the nature of the unconscious Jung was encountering with his patients. When Jung's own discoveries conflicted with Freud's theories, he hoped Freud would adapt his theories. That wasn't to be.

Now on his own, Jung was forced to rely exclusively on his own observations of the psyche. For the first time, he began to look at his patients' dreams without any preconceptions about their meaning. At the same time, he began an exploration of his own unconscious processes. In doing so, he tried to deal directly with what he encountered, without the protection of Freudian dogma to categorize his experience. In his spiritual autobiography, *Memories, Dreams, Reflections* (hereafter *MDM*), he remembers what it was like for him in those days:

> After the parting of the ways with Freud, a period of inner uncertainty began for me. It would be no exaggeration to call it a state of disorientation. . . . I avoided all theoretical points of view and simply helped the patients to understand the dream-images by themselves, without application of rules and theories. Soon I realized that it was right to take the dreams in this way as the basis of interpretation, for that is how dreams are intended. (1)

A few pages later, he adds this:

> I lived as if under constant pressure. At times this became so strong that I suspected there was some psychic disturbance in myself. Therefore, I twice went over all the details of my entire life, with particular attention to childhood memories; for I thought there might be something in my past which I could not see and which might possibly be a cause for this disturbance. But this retrospection led to nothing but a fresh acknowledgment of my ignorance. Thereupon I said to myself, "Since I know nothing at all, I shall simply do whatever occurs to me." Thus I consciously submitted to the impulses of the unconscious. (2)

In order to keep some stability in his life during this period, he kept regular office hours with patients, and spent a normal amount of time with his wife and children. When the energy from the unconscious grew too overpowering, he would do Yoga exercises, which helped somewhat in containing the energy. The rest of the time, he wandered alone in the alien terrain of the unconscious. Here's how he described his feelings in encountering the unconscious:

> An incessant stream of fantasies had been released, and I did my best not to lose my head but to find some way to understand these strange things. I stood helpless before an alien world . . . I was living in a state of constant tension; often I felt as if gigantic blocks of stone were tumbling down upon me. One thunderstorm followed another. My enduring these storms was a question of brute strength. . . . To the extent that I managed to translate the emotions into images--that is to say, to find the images which were concealed in the emotions--I was inwardly calmed and reassured. Had I left those images hidden in the emotions, I might have been torn to pieces by them . . . as a result of my experiment I learned how helpful it can be, from the therapeutic point of view, to find the particular images which lie behind the emotions. (3)

From 1913 to 1917, Jung lived in this symbolic world. As time passed, and he weathered the storms that raged within him, he gradually developed a psychic center where it was always calm, even during the storms.

Finally, "the stream of fantasies ebbed away" [4], and he took stock of what he had discovered about the bizarre region he had been surveying.

Opinions have varied as to whether this period marked a true psychotic break in Jung's life. In his important book, *The Ego and the Dynamic Ground,* [5] philosopher Michael Washburn differentiates psychotic episodes from what he terms "Regression in the Service of Transcendence" ("RIST", clearly contrasting it with Freud's concept of Regression in the Service of the Ego). Washburn argues that in the spiritual journey a point is reached when the ego must be transcended and, paradoxically enough, that can only happen by regressing to an pre-ego state of mind. There are four stages to this process: (1) Withdrawal from the World; (2) Encounter with the Personal Unconscious (which for Washburn eventually activates the instinctual/archetypal unconscious as well); (3) Regeneration in Spirit; and (4) Integration. The key element for Washburn is that this is a process of health, not disease. And clearly Jung's "dark night of the soul" included a forced withdrawal from the world, a deep encounter with the unconscious, and eventually a regeneration of spirit. The results of this time were integrated slowly within Jung over the remainder of his life.

Gnosticism as Analytic Psychology's Precursor

Jung realized that his conclusions about the nature of the psyche would likely be regarded as outlandish by other psychologists, even by the small number of psychoanalysts who acknowledged that there was such a thing as an unconscious mind. He needed some support for his discoveries and turned to history for that support.

Jung also discusses this problem in *Memories, Dreams, Reflections*:

> I had to find evidence for the historical prefiguration of my inner experiences. That is to say, I had to ask myself, "Where have my particular premises already occurred in history?" If I had not succeeded in finding such evidence, I would never have been able to substantiate my ideas . . .Between 1918 and 1926 I had seriously studied the Gnostic writers, for they too had been confronted with the primal world of the unconscious and had dealt with its contents, with images that were obviously contaminated with the world of instinct. Just how they understood these images remains difficult to say, in view of the paucity of the accounts--which, moreover, mostly stem from their opponents, the Church Fathers. It seems to me highly unlikely that they had a psychological conception of them. [6]

Just who were these Gnostics in whose lives and beliefs Jung found prefigurations for his ideas? In fact there was no single group or single set of ideas which could be termed Gnostic. The Gnostics were composed of Christians of the 1st and 2nd century A.D., with widely divergent beliefs. However, their Christianity itself is enough to separate them from the Neoplatonists, who were largely "pagan" and who reacted strongly against many of the tenets of Christianity. Today we discuss Gnostics as a group largely because of their common opposition to the form of Christianity that won out during this period and went on to become the major force of the Western World.

However, if there was a single unifying belief shared by the Gnostics, it was a belief in "Gnosis"; i.e., a belief that religious truth could be directly perceived by the individual. In other words, you and I could be like Christ. In contrast, traditional Christianity stressed the separation between Christ and man, just as Judaism has stressed the separation of Jehovah and man. Mainstream Christianity taught that Christ had been fully God, but had allowed himself to be born a man, in order to unite God and man within himself. Only in this way could he suffer and die as a man, and thus atone for the original sin of pride committed by Adam and Eve in the Garden of Eden.

By his sacrifice, Christ provided the possibility of redemption for sinful humanity. We could best follow Christ's example by living a life in accordance with the ethical teachings he left us; which were summed up in the Golden Rule: "love thy neighbor as thyself." The Gnostics, on the other hand, believed that we could best follow Christ's example not only by living ethically, but by trying like Christ to experience God within ourselves. The Gnostic ideal was for direct religious experience, mystical experience. We, too, could experience the numinous!

Thus Gnostics--and I stress that they were many and varied in their beliefs--were involved in an exploration of the unconscious forces of their own psyches (though it is doubtful they were aware of the psychological implications of their exploration.)

In his own exploration of the unconscious, Jung had found that the energies of the collective unconscious were so powerful that his emotions were in danger of overwhelming him. He had to convert these unconscious energies into images in order to survive. Because the Gnostics were investigating the same territory, they also found it necessary to convert the primordial energy they encountered into images.

As a consequence, the Gnostic teachings were largely symbolic. They presented mythological stories of creation, loss and redemption, which stood in opposition to the traditional biblical stories that dealt with the same topics. Unlike Jung, they didn't yet understand the symbolic nature of their stories and treated them as literal. This is still the most common danger for anyone who ventures into the collective unconscious.

The Disparagement of the Body

In general, Christianity exalted the spirit and reviled the body. Because of their goal of direct spiritual experience, this tendency was even more pronounced among Gnostics. They postulated a highest god--Abraxas--who was above all dualities and could be discussed only in terms of what he was not. Below Abraxas was an inferior god who created the world. The world he created was not only inferior, but actually evil. It was our duty to recognize that our true home was the spirit and separate ourselves from its inferior vessel: the body. So there was a thorough-going disparagement of the world and the body in Gnosticism.

Perhaps I could pause here to say a few words about this trap, for it's a trap that catches nearly all of us who engage in a spiritual journey at one time or another. As with so many other of his brilliant discoveries, Jung saw deeper than others here, too. He continually stressed that the archetypes, which were the building blocks of the collective unconscious, had two equal and opposite aspects:

(1) as *primordial images* (his original term for archetypes); and

(2) as *instinctual behaviors.*

This two-headed identity of the archetypes is nothing mysterious; it's just an acknowledgment that the essentially formless archetypes have to be channeled through the human mind and body. There's really only two ways we are capable of channeling these most basic of all psychic structures:

(1) inside our minds, in order to structure our perception of the world; (and it's important to realize that these inner images don't have to be visual; they can be auditory, kinesthetic, etc.); or

(2) outside, in the world, as behavior toward the people and things we encounter in the world.

We experience the world and we act in the world. Archetypes are structures, but essentially formless structures until they take form in our lives as images or behaviors.

In consequence of our very humanity, spirit and instinct are joined within us. Unfortunately, most spiritual traditions, including the Gnostics, try to exalt the spirit at the expense of the instincts. Jung was wise enough to realize that instinct and spirit are two aspects of a single thing; as such, both have to be acknowledged and reconciled. It is no more possible to separate spirit from instinct than to lift ourselves off the ground by grabbing the seat of our own pants.

Unlike so many others in both spiritual and psychological traditions, Jung didn't regard the separation of mind and body, spirit and instinct, as a tragic flaw. Instead he regarded this seeming duality as an organic unity. Just as a tree needs both deep roots in the earth and leafy branches stretching toward the sky, we need both instincts to root us in the basic facts of our animal nature and spirituality to remind us of the numinous possibilities alive at every moment in the world around us. Both are integral parts of our essential humanity.

Jung stands nearly alone in this attitude. The three great modern religions (Christianity, Buddhism, and Islam) all preach in one way or another that the body is evil; the wants and needs of the body must be sacrificed in order to properly honor the spirit. (In contrast, the older religions like Judaism, Hinduism, Shintoism, etc., are more tolerant of the body.) Most esoteric spiritual and occult traditions have the same split. Most seem to think that the body can and should be transcended.

Freud's great achievement was in pointing out that it is impossible to ignore our instinctual nature without doing damage to our psyches. Freud saw all energy as basically sexual; i.e., instinctual. In Freud's view, the basis of civilization lies in mankind's ability to put curbs on that instinctual energy. But doing so causes a conflict within each of us, a conflict which has no real solution within Freud's framework.

In Freud's view, the best we can do is develop healthy defenses against this animal side of our nature, with the healthiest such defense probably sublimation; i.e., the channeling of "lower" energy into "higher" forms. But all we are really doing is providing an outlet for instinctual energy so that we don't reach a breaking point; we have in no way reconciled the two opposing sides of our personalities.

Similarly, in recent days, Ken Wilbur, who is transpersonal psychology's most eloquent spokesman, has called Jung's linkage of spirit and instinct the "Pre-Trans-Fallacy." Here Wilbur is expressing the conventional wisdom of the esoteric spiritual tradition which believe that there is a lower part of our nature (i.e., the **sub**conscious) which needs to be transcended in order to reach a higher (i.e., the **super**conscious.)

This is a critical problem, one which we will have to return to later. It's certainly a problem which neither traditional Christianity nor the Gnostics solved successfully. Though the Neoplatonists also didn't fully solve this problem, we'll see later that they came closer to a solution than anyone before, or after, until Jung.

The Paradoxical Nature of the Psyche

We've seen that Jung felt isolated in his view of the psyche (in fact in his view of the entire world, since Jung almost alone among modern thinkers saw the world without and the world within meeting in the conscious awareness of the individual.) He knew the dangers involved when the human mind tries to examine itself. When the mind thinks about the mind, we become involved in a vicious circle, a self-referential loop which can lead to paradoxical conclusions.

Because he was involved in just such an examination, Jung discovered many paradoxes inherent in the psyche: e.g., that we contained an instinctual drive (hence part of our supposedly lower nature) to fulfil our spiritual destiny (hence part of our higher nature). He described that drive alternately as "individuation" (in terms of its importance for individual development) and as the "transcendent function", (with its emphasis on a need for a wholeness which transcends individuality.) That's quite a paradox.

As if that wasn't enough, he found that each of us contains an unconscious complement to our conscious personality, which he termed the Shadow because, like a physical shadow, it appears when a person is seen in too great a light. The Shadow seems to represent everything we regard as vile and despicable, everything which we deny and avoid. So a desire for too much light, too much spirituality, creates darkness, or instinctuality. Again a paradox.

Balanced between the extremes of our conscious personality and this unconscious complement, between the Ego and the Shadow, lies a personality of total wholeness, as close as each of us can come to divinity, which Jung termed the Self (with a capital "S" to differentiate it from the commonplace use of the term). This Self is not only the center between extremes, it appears to also be both the goal of individuation, and the self-regulatory process by which we attain that goal; i.e., the transcendent function. So higher and lower, process and goal, conscious and unconscious, are all united within us.

That's paradox enough for anyone to consider and exactly the kind of thing that made Jung wonder if perhaps he was just a madman projecting his fantasies out onto the world. If he wasn't, he knew that others had to have visited this same territory before and he should be able to find evidence of their search. That's why the Gnostics were so important to Jung. Their mythologies, which were condemned as crazy heresies by the established church, were obviously symbolic representations of the same paradoxes which Jung had encountered.

His discovery of the Gnostic mythologies proved to Jung that he wasn't crazy; the world was really as exotic as he had found it to be. However, as we've seen, the Gnostics couldn't reconcile the paradoxical nature of reality and instead condemned the world, the body, our instinctual nature as evil.

Now, if Jung is right, and the higher and the lower are really a single entity, it should be impossible to cut off the lower and still find the higher.

Just as an illustration, imagine a piece of rope held vertically. Let's cut off that inferior lower end of it. The rope that remains still has both an upper end and a lower end. No matter how many times we cut it, the rope still has two ends. However, if we cut it too many times, there's almost no rope left. That's the circumstance in which we find ourselves if we condemn our instinctual nature and simply try to cut it off from our lives. It doesn't go away; it can't. Instead we find ourselves becoming smaller and smaller people, until there's not enough left of us to accomplish anything worthwhile in our lives. And that's sad.

Plotinus and the Founding of Neoplatonism

Having discussed the importance of Gnosticism as a precursor to Jungian psychology, and the limits of Gnosticism, with its condemnation of the body and instinct, it is finally time to discuss Neoplatonism itself. As the name implies, Neoplatonism was a new formulation of the philosophy of Plato. However,

Neoplatonist philosophers did not consider that they were saying anything new; they felt that they were just developing ideas which were already in Plato, either explicitly or implicitly. In fact, they didn't see any dramatic split between the ideas of Plato, with his world of ideal forms, and Aristotle, with his emphasis on the actual forms we encounter in nature, which we do today. To the Neoplatonists, both Plato and Aristotle were talking about the same thing. It is in the Neoplatonist's ability to see a unity, where perhaps there was none, that their greatness lies.

I would imagine that it is because the Neoplatonists were philosophers, not latent psychologists, that Jung did not regard them as precursors of his own work. Gnostics and alchemists spoke in symbols, Neoplatonists in rational ideas. But different routes often arrive at the same destination.

Because the Neoplatonists were pagan, they never disparaged the body to the same extent as the Christians: both traditional and Gnostic. Though they believed in the traditional Platonic goal of reason leading to the ideal, they did not condemn matter and the body out of hand, like the Christians. Instead, in trying to reconcile body and spirit, they found themselves involved in a paradox which they struggled over three hundred years to resolve.

Let me give you a very brief history of Neoplatonism. Plotinus, who lived in the 3rd century, A.D. is generally regarded as the founder of Neoplatonism. He was born in Egypt, traveled widely in Syria and Persia, and settled in Rome. He was the first clear expositor of the central theme of Neoplatonism, which I'm calling "The Stairway to Heaven" in this paper.

In brief, this is the idea that there is a single undifferentiated, divine One, and everything else in existence came about as an "emanation" from this One. We can substitute the word God for the One, as long as we don't attribute any anthropomorphic qualities to God. It's harder to find a word that fully captures what they meant by "emanate." It doesn't mean simply "create" in the normal sense of most creation myths. The emanations are not separate from the One; they partake of the One. They may be diffuse, but they are still a part of the One. Radiate is a close parallel, as in the sun radiates light.

There is a hierarchy of emanations, or levels, that lead down from the divine to the mundane. (The Gnostics had a very similar concept in their mythologies.) The first level of emanations is Nous or Supreme Intelligence. This is the level of Plato's divine forms, and Jung's archetypes. The second level is that of the World Soul. The last level is the world itself. It's up to man, by the exercise of philosophy, to recognize the existence of these higher levels and gradually rise up them until he is able to rejoin with the One.

In this early days of Neoplatonism, there was a disparagement of the lowest level--the World itself--that was almost as extreme as the Gnostics. However, there was already a recognition that the world is holographic, i.e., each emanation, since it comes from the One and partakes of the One, must in some way also contain the One. Therefore, the instincts can't be totally evil, since somehow they must also contain the divine. This is the key recognition by the Neoplatonists that brings them closer to Jung than the Gnostics or the alchemists.

However, this holographic view wasn't really stressed by Plotinus. His emphasis was on rising up the ladder toward the divine.

Iamblichus and the Development of Neoplatonism

The next great Neoplatonic thinker was the Syrian Iamblichus, who was born the same year Plotinus died. He vastly elaborated Plotinus' concept of the three-way Stairway to Heaven, in large part drawing on the Pythagorean idea of the divinity of number. Iamblichus divided the level of Supreme Intelligence into two separate triads. The level of World Soul was divided into another triad. Each such division had categories and sub-categories galore.

While this elaborate system is fascinating in itself, I'm less concerned with the details of the system than I am with the central contribution of Iamblichus: each of these categories was assigned a god or goddess who personified the characteristics associated with that category. These hundreds of divinities interceded in the life of mankind and the world and could be addressed through prayers and offerings.

This led to the second great concept of Neoplatonism: the practice of theurgy (from the Greek *theos* or god, and *ergon* or work; thus the *god work*). This was the ritual enactment of episodes in the life of a god in order to join with that god.

This might seem like a reversion to a more primitive belief system, but it also brings Neoplatonism closer to the world of the psyche as pictured by Jung. Under Plotinus, we had an essentially intellectual philosophical system, which had little room for the day-to-day concerns of ordinary men and women. The task of the philosopher was to recognize the transitory nature of physical reality in order to peer beneath the veil at the mystery that lay underneath. That's quite marvelous, and half of the story, but only half.

With Iamblichus' addition of the gods who represented each category of emanation, a more human system began to emerge which recognized that men and women need more than intellectual solutions to the paradoxes of life.

Proclus and the Culmination of Neoplatonism

The high-point of Neoplatonism was reached in Athens in the late 5th century by the man I consider Neoplatonism's greatest philosopher: Proclus. Proclus was born in Constantinople, studied in both Alexandria and Athens, and was the head of the Neoplatonic School of Athens until his death.

In order to get a feeling for the importance of Proclus, we might think of him as being to Neoplatonism what Bach was to Baroque music. In neither case, would we emphasize revolutionary creativity, though both were creative geniuses of a very high order. In both cases, an entire tradition reached its peak and found full expression in their work. Bach encapsulated Baroque music so perfectly that, after Bach, there was really no need for any further development of Baroque music. The way was prepared for "Classical" music.

Similarly, Proclus brought together all the disparate threads of Neoplatonic thought, not only in his philosophy, but in his life. Proclus lived his philosophy, as Bach lived his music, and as Jung lived his psychology. There was a wholeness, a balance to Proclus' version of Neoplatonism that was lacking in its earlier proponents and which was never again recaptured in its later adherents. In his attempt to bring all of Neoplatonism together into a single system of both thought and life, Proclus was brilliant enough to separate out two central ideas.

(1) *The Stairway of Heaven which leads from God down to man, and back up again, is holographic at every level*; i.e., even if the world of men and women is inferior to God and his world, we each contain that world in some part within us. At the lowest level of instinctual nature, we are still capable of experiencing divinity; all nature is holy.

This is an amazingly modern concept. I don't know of a truly clear presentation of it until the twentieth century, when religious historian Mircea Eliade discussed his concept of the Sacred and the Profane. Eliade said that "by manifesting the sacred, any object becomes something else, yet it continues to remain itself." In other words, everything is both sacred and profane. Something becomes sacred, numinous, when we see it as numinous. It is the sacred inside us which is able to experience the sacred in something outside us. This recognition lead Proclus to the second great Neoplatonic idea.

(2) *The practice of theurgy is above all human wisdom.* Proclus saw the world as filled with divinity. By that, he did not mean just some ambiguous life force which permeated everything; he meant that there were clearly defined gods who, in total, represented every aspect of

both the Sacred and the Profane. By interacting with those divinities in an appropriate ritual manner, man could awaken similar qualities within himself and gradually advance up the Stairway toward the One.

Again this is an amazingly modern idea, not a reversion to a primitive belief system. Jung was to echo similar thoughts when he said that the gods have become diseases. By that he meant that, since we have denied the more-than-human forces of the psyche which we previously regarded as gods, the gods express themselves in the only way possible to them: through highly specific diseases of our bodies and souls.

Primitive man populated the world with gods and goddesses who personified the different aspects of reality. Modern psychologists have come to understand that the gods were actually aspects of our own psyches which we projected out onto the world. However, Jung saw deeper; he insisted that our awareness of the psychological origin of the gods in no way invalidates their more-than-human numinousity. We are still better off regarding them as gods than in thinking that we can dismiss them as intellectual constructs.

Living fifteen hundred years ago, Proclus did not, of course, have the psychological acumen of a Jung. However, he did understand that the gods are not only outside us, but also live within us. By constructing rituals to interact with the gods as they present themselves in the world, we can access the corresponding godlike parts of our own deepest personalities. This is a far more sophisticated concept than that held by primitive man, who conducted ceremonies to propitiate or honor the gods. It is also far more sophisticated than that held by modern man, who dismisses the gods as merely intellectual creations.

The Importance of Neoplatonism in Our Own Lives

There is very little more that needs to be said at that point, except to try and bring some of this down to earth, and discuss what it means in our individual lives, and how we can use this knowledge to aid us in our own journeys of individuation.

First, the concept that there are definable levels between the sacred and the profane is important. Individuation is a long, difficult journey that takes a lifetime (or more) to complete. It's very easy to lose our bearings along the way. It makes an immeasurable difference if, when things get tough, we are able to identify where we are on the journey. It helps to recognize that perhaps we are having a difficult time in our lives because we have reached a stage that is difficult for everyone.

Jungian psychology provides us with at least two useful models of those levels or stages of development:

(1) The model of the archetypes of development: the Shadow, the Anima/Animus, and the Self; and

(2) The model of the alchemical coniunctios: the union within the mind, the union of mind and body, and the union with the totality of the world.

When we recognize that what we're experiencing is a Shadow problem, or a characteristic encounter with the Anima or Animus, we feel less lonely and isolated. There's a reason why we're struggling. Our suffering acquires a meaning that gives it dignity.

Another useful model I have drawn on frequently in my own life is the Hero's Journey as presented by Joseph Campbell in *The Hero with a Thousand Faces.* [7] Many a time, I have been able to recognize difficulties associated with "crossing the boundary", confronting the "guardians of the gate", etc. That recognition made my situation less frightening and more meaningful.

Neoplatonism originated the concept of a progressive, evolutionary path, which now permeates our thinking. However, Neoplatonism had a second element which is missing in the modern concept of progress, with its insistence on higher and farther, better and richer. This is the holographic concept that at each step of the journey, we have the potential to experience the One that is the goal of the journey.

Anyone who has ever played "Snakes and Ladders" (or any of the modern computer arcade versions such as

"Donkey Kong") is familiar with this phenomenon. If you land on the right square in "Snakes and Ladders," you can climb directly up a ladder to a higher level. But step on the wrong square and you can ride a snake all the way back to the beginning.

Similarly, in our path of individuation, we are capable at any moment of experiencing enlightenment, a "satori" as it is termed in Zen, an "epiphany" to James Joyce. At any time, we can see the sacred in the profane because everything in our lives is pregnant with meaning if we would only see it. Again, we owe that recognition to Neoplatonism.

Finally, Proclus insisted that we need theurgy to mediate between the material and the spiritual. Jungian psychology warns equally against the inflation that follows trying to swallow an archetype, and the depression that follows the archetype swallowing us. Unfortunately, there is no easy way to proceed along the path of development without experiencing both inflation and depression. We have to encounter the gods in order to assimilate their human possibilities into our personality.

It would be nice if life wasn't so difficult. It would have been easier if Adam and Eve could have stayed in Eden, yet mankind could still have progressed along the path of consciousness that would lead eventually to a Christ consciousness. But that's not possible; there's a price to pay for consciousness. What is possible is to structure the encounters with the gods so that we are protected from their more-than-human energy.

Jung warned of the dangers for Westerners of taking the Eastern paths which deny both the physical world and the products of the unconscious as illusionary. Something denied doesn't go away; it builds up in the unconscious, sometimes to lethal proportions. Jung instead recommended working with dreams and Active Imagination.

In my experience, the former is a perfect example of theurgy. The unconscious presents the gods (i.e., the archetypes) to us in symbolic dramas unique to each of us. Jung insisted that a self-regulatory process protects us in our work with dreams. After working with over 15,000 of my own dreams over the last two decade, I've got experiential evidence that Jung is right. When I'm not ready to deal with the implications of a dream in my life, I can't understand it no matter how much I try. When I'm ready, the understanding is there. But, regardless of my level of understanding, the actual process of engaging with the dreams accelerates the process of my own growth. So dream work is a wonderful method of practicing theurgy.

Here's how Jung described his second method: Active Imagination:

> Take the unconscious in one of its handiest forms, say a spontaneous fantasy, a dream, an irrational mood, an affect, or something of the kind, and operate with it. Give it your special attention, concentrate on it, and observe its alterations objectively. Spare no effort to devote yourself to this task, follow the subsequent transformations of the spontaneous fantasy attentively and carefully. Above all, don't let anything from outside, that does not belong, get into it, for the fantasy-image has "everything it needs." In this way, one is certain of not interfering by conscious caprice and of giving the unconscious a free hand. [8]

In my experience, Active Imagination is nowhere near so safe or infallible a process as dream work. When we "give the unconscious a free hand," as Jung suggests, the unconscious doesn't always provide us with honest answers. Like many other methods of encountering the unconscious, Active Imagination can be deceptive. Mercurius frequently plays games with us, and it takes a great deal of experience to separate truth from falsity in this encounter. However, when aware of its dangers, Active Imagination can provide counsel unavailable to us in dreams alone. The most important way to avoid the pitfalls is to remember the "active" participation by consciousness which is implied in the phrase "active imagination", and not simply allow the unconscious to have sway.

Jung encouraged other methods of structuring the unconscious, such as drawing, painting or sculpting our dreams, drawing mandalas that express our state of wholeness (or lack thereof) at any particular point, etc. These are all useful tools that help protect us from the overwhelming force of the unconscious.

Unfortunately, none of these methods involve ritual, and it was the ritual encounter with the gods which Proclus saw as the supreme contribution of theurgy. Jung himself realized how much we need ritual in our lives. Traditionally, it has been provided within our religious lives. Our religions have provided sacraments and rituals for every important event in our lives.

However, religion no longer occupies center stage in the lives of many of us, and there is very little ritual left in modern life. This means that when we do meet the gods, we meet them unprepared. And that's dangerous. So, if our culture no longer offers us such rituals, we have to construct them ourselves. This is what Jung meant that we said that each of us has to discover our myth. What is unique in our time is that collective rituals are no longer sufficient, we each have to construct rituals that fit our individual lives.

The central issue of our day is how we can construct rituals which can serve both individually and collectively. That's another way of saying that we need a new "living symbol" in our lives. Over sixty years ago,

Jung discussed the role which the individual can play in bringing a new archetypal symbol into existence:

> Only the passionate yearning of a highly developed mind, for which the traditional symbol is no longer the unified expression of the rational and the irrational, of the highest and the lowest, can create a new symbol.
> But precisely because the new symbol is born of man's highest spiritual aspirations and must at the same time spring from the deepest roots of his being, it cannot be a one-sided product of the most highly differentiated mental functions, but must derive equally from the lowest and most primitive levels of the psyche. [9]

The Neoplatonists struggled for three hundred years with that problem. Proclus was able to find an inner harmony through theurgy, but the rituals he engaged in were not powerful enough to capture the general population, and Neoplatonism died out. Now, fifteen hundred years later, we are struggling with the same issue once more.

Those closest to the unconscious are usually the first to experience any new aspect of the gods. In that light, let me close with some excerpts from a poem by Wallace Stevens called "Notes Toward a Supreme Fiction." [10] More than nearly any other twentieth century poet,

Wallace Stevens struggled to reconcile the world that exists outside us with the world that exists in each of our minds. This is the same issue with which both Jung and the Neoplatonists struggled. I hope that the following at least offer hints toward how we can reconcile the two and advance up the Stairway to Heaven:

First, maybe the most important tip Stevens can offer:

You must become an ignorant man again
And see the sun again with an ignorant eye . . .

Here's the trap that those of us in the late twentieth century have fallen into, when we try to dismiss the gods with logic:

. . . The death of one god is the death of all . . .

Here's a central insight of both Stevens and Jung:

. . . There was a myth before the myth began.

Now here finally is as close as Stevens comes to providing an answer, perhaps as close as any of us can come:

. . . Perhaps
The truth depends on a walk around a lake,
A composing as the body tires, a stop
To see hepatica, a stop to watch
A definition growing certain and
A wait within that certainty, a rest
In the swags of pine-trees bordering the lake.
Perhaps there are times of inherent excellence.
. . . Perhaps there are moments of awakening.

REFERENCES

1. C. G. Jung, *Memories, Dreams, Reflections,* revised edition (New York: Pantheon Books, 1973), pp. 170-171.

2. *C. G. Jung,* Memories, Dreams, Reflections, *p. 173.*

3. *C. G. Jung,* Memories, Dreams, Reflections, *pp. 176-177.*

4. *C. G. Jung,* Memories, Dreams, Reflections, *p. 206.*

5. *Michael Washburn,* The Ego and the Dynamic Ground: A Transpersonal Theory of Human Development *(New York: SUNY Press, 1995).*

6. *C. G. Jung,* Memories, Dreams, Reflections, *pp. 200-201.*

7. Joseph Campbell, *The Hero with a Thousand Faces,* 2nd edition (Princeton: Princeton University Press, 1968).

8. C. G. Jung, CW14: *Mysterium Coniunctionis,* 2nd edition (Princeton: Princeton University Press, 1970) par. 749.

9. C. G. Jung, CW6: *Psychological Types* (Princeton: Princeton University Press, 1971), par. 823-824.

10. Wallace Stevens, *The Palm at the End of the Mind* (New York: Vintage Books, 1972), pp. 207-234.

THE CASE OF THE MISSING THIRD

How is it that form arises out of chaos? In attempting to deal with this primary question, time and again a "missing third" is posited that lies between extremes. The problem of the "missing third" can be traced through nearly the entire history of thought. The form it takes, the problems that arise from it, the solutions suggested for resolving it, are each representative of an age.

This paper traces the issue from Plato and Parmenides in the 4th - 5th centuries, B.C.; to Neoplatonism in the 3rd - 5th centuries; to Locke and Descartes in the 17th century; on to Berkeley and Kant in the 18th century; Fechner and Wundt in the 19th century; to behaviorism, Gestalt psychology, and Jungian psychology, early in the 20th century, ethology and cybernetics later in the 20th century, then culminates late in the 20th century, with chaos theory.

In *Process and Reality,* Alfred North Whitehead said that "The safest general characterization of the European philosophical tradition is that it consists of a series of footnotes to Plato" (Whitehead, 1929, 39). So our proper starting point is Plato.

4TH - 5TH CENTURY, B.C.

Parmenides' 3rd Man Argument Against Plato's Ideals

In Plato's dialogue *Parmenides,* a young Socrates presents his theory that the "things" we think of as real in the physical world necessarily acquire their form from a world of idealized "forms," commonly known today as Platonic "ideas" or "ideals." Aristotle used the term "Third Man" for Parmenides' concise argument against Socrates' (that is, Plato's) model.

Parmenides argued that when Socrates examined a number of things that appeared to have a common characteristic, such as largeness, Socrates concluded that largeness must itself be a single thing. But if he then added largeness to the set of large things, then there must be a new characteristic which they all share. We might call that largeness-2. But the process can continue indefinitely, with a largeness-3, largeness-4, etc. (Cornford, 1957). So any attempt to find ideal forms ends up denying those ideal forms since each ideal form has an infinite number of versions.

In the same dialogue, Parmenides presents his answer to such problems: that there is a single underlying principle of being, "whether one is or is not, one and the others in relation to themselves and one another, all of them, in every way, are and are not, and appear to be and appear not to be" (Comford, 1957). In other words, the only way to get out of the infinite regress is to realize that there is no multiplicity, that all is one.

Parmenides' disciple Zeno wrote a book whose object, according to Plato: " . . . was to defend the system of Parmenides by attacking the common conceptions of things" (Heath, 1981). The Neoplatonist philosopher Proclus (of whom we'll hear more later) said that the book "elaborated forty different paradoxes following from the assumption of plurality and motion, all of them apparently based on the difficulties deriving from an analysis of the continuum" (Gillispie, 1980). Aristotle preserved four of these paradoxes; fragments of several others survive from other sources. Though all present the problem of the missing third to one degree or another, two do so most explicitly:

In "Dichotomy," Zeno argues that a mid-point always lies between any starting and ending point. But that mid-point can be considered as a new ending point and, therefore a new mid-point can be identified between it and the starting point. And so on.

In the famous race between Achilles and the Tortoise, if the Tortoise is given a lead to begin, Achilles can never catch him because, by the time Achilles reaches the Tortoise's starting point, the Tortoise will have moved farther. When Achilles reaches that point, the Tortoise will have move again. And so on.

Why do these paradoxes occur? Zeno would agree with Parmenides that the problem is the assumption that time and space are divisible, when, in actuality, space and time are each indivisible concepts, impossible to break into parts. So, at this point, there seems no possible solution: structure and form must come from somewhere, yet if the come from without, then one is led into a paradox. Of course, if one then assumes, like Zeno and Parmenides, that "all is one," the problem has simply been ignored, not answered.

3RD - 5TH CENTURY

Neoplatonism: Plotinus, Iamblichus, and Proclus

As the name implies, Neoplatonism was a new formulation of the philosophy of Plato. However, Neoplatonist philosophers did not consider that they were saying anything new; they felt that they were just developing ideas which were already in Plato, either explicitly or implicitly. In fact, they didn't see any dramatic split between the ideas of Plato, with his world of ideal forms, and Aristotle, with his emphasis on the actual forms we encounter in nature.

A brief history of Neoplatonism necessarily includes three figures: Plotinus, Iamblichus, and Proclus. Plotinus, who lived in the 3rd century, A.D. was the founder of

Neoplatonism. He was born in Egypt, traveled widely in Syria and Persia, and settled in Rome. He was the first clear expositor of the central theme of Neoplatonism. In brief, this is the idea that there is a single undifferentiated, divine One, and everything else in existence came about as an "emanation" from this One. We can substitute the word God for the One, as long as we don't attribute any anthropomorphic qualities to God. It's harder to find a word that fully captures what the Neoplatonists meant by "emanate." They didn't mean "create" in the normal sense of most creation myths. The emanations are not separate from the One; they partake of the One. They may be diffuse, but they are still a part of the One. Radiate is a close parallel, as in the sun radiates light. This idea of emanations is what allows the Neoplatonists to reconcile Parmenides' One with Plato's Ideals, without falling into an infinite regress.

They argued that there is a graduated hierarchy of levels of the emanations that leads down from the divine to the mundane. (The Gnostics had a very similar concept in their mythologies.) The first level of emanations is Nous or Supreme Intelligence. This is the level of Plato's ideal forms. The second level is that of the World Soul. The last level is the world itself. Though each of these levels is different and progressively further from the One, each is still in part composed of the One. So from an undifferentiated One emerges three levels.

The next great Neoplatonic thinker was the Syrian Iamblichus, who was born the same year Plotinus died. He vastly elaborated Plotinus' concept of the three-way path down from the Nous to the World, in large part drawing on the Pythagorean idea of the divinity of number. Iamblichus divided the level of Supreme Intelligence into two separate triads. The level of World Soul was divided into another triad. Each such division had categories and sub-categories galore. But the idea of a triad held throughout.

The high-point of Neoplatonism was reached in Athens in the late 5th century by Proclus. Proclus was born in Constantinople, studied in both Alexandria and Athens, and was the head of the Neoplatonic School of Athens until his death. He took the idea of a hierarchy of emanations from the One to its limit and argued that Iamblichus' complex *hierarchy was holographic at every level,* since the emanations of the One necessarily partook of the One. Now, of course, he didn't call it holographic in the same sense that, for example, neurophysiologist Karl Pribram talks of the world as being holographic. But Proclus did argue that it was possible at any level to have direct apprehension of the One.

Where Plato argued that the things of the world were pale copies of ideal forms, and Parmenides and his disciple Zeno argued that everything in nature constituted a single, indivisible whole, the Neoplatonists accepted both. They were able to reconcile these two opposing views by positing a hierarchy between the One and the World, each stage of which was potentially holographic with the One. To put this into a two-stage form (rather than the three-stages of Neoplatonism) that sounds less "mystical," and anticipates later views, we might say that:

- The organizing principles of experiential realities are to be found in logical realities.
- The organizing principles of logical realities are to be found in first principles outside of those realities.

[Note that I'm indebted to Robert Porter, Ph.D. for this concise formulation].

Of course, this was not clear yet when the Neoplatonists formulated their structure. Let us now move forward over a thousand years to a quaternity of philosophers who bring new views to the table.

17TH - 18TH CENTURY

Locke, Descartes, Berkeley, and Kant

Seventeenth century British philosopher John Locke was the first since Plato to offer a new theory of ideas. He argued that the mind, at birth, was a *tabula rasa* (blank slate) upon which sensory experience wrote. We accumulated sensations which were stored as simple ideas. The mind combined those simple ideas into more complex ideas. But all ideas were directly or indirectly from sensory experience of the world.

At roughly the same time, in France, mathematician and philosopher Rene Descartes proclaimed his credo of "*Cogito, ergo sum* " ("I think, therefore I am"). In the eighteenth century, British philosopher Bishop George Berkeley took Descartes' concept to its logical extreme and turned Locke's model on its head. Instead of the primacy of the world, Berkeley asserted the primacy of the mind: *all we ever know are our thoughts.* We have no proof that any world exists outside those thoughts. (Though Berkeley allowed it to exist by asserting that the world was a thought in the mind of God).

Clearly there was a need for a new "third" to resolve this paradox. This was provided in 1781, when Immanuel Kant published his *Critique of Pure Reason.* Kant agreed with Berkeley that all we can ever really experience are our thoughts, but sided with Locke in asserting that there actually is a world outside us. The reconciliation between the two seemingly irreconcilable positions lay in the fact that the human mind is far from a blank slate at birth. Instead it contains inherent "categories" through which we filter sensory data. We can think of these "categories" as in some way related to Plato's ideas. Instead of existing in some unknown location outside of the world we live in, however, they exist in the mind. Kant said that judgement consisted of taking in sensory data through the lens of these inherent structures, then applying logic to reach a conclusion. In Kant's words "thoughts without content are empty, and intuitions without concepts are blind" (Reese, 1980, 276-80).

Though we might never be able to experience *das ding an sich* (the thing in itself), our minds are themselves structured much as the world is structured, and contain necessarily true categories with which we perceive the world. Kant's categories formed the missing third that lay between the mind and the world. Basically, Kant was the first to state explicitly the first of the two laws we presented earlier: "The organizing principles of experiential realities are to be found in logical realities."

If these "categories" sound unlikely, substitute the word "attractor" and see if it becomes more palatable. We will later discuss Walter Freeman's discovery of sensory attractors.

19TH CENTURY

Fechner, Wundt, and James

German philosopher Gustav Fechner was an interesting study in contrasts, and his work reflected those contrasts. Throughout his life he was pulled between the twin poles of mind and matter, in his case expressed by his interest in both metaphysics and science. His early work was first in physiology, then in physics. He experienced a crisis in mid-life, where he became ill and withdrew from the world. His earlier work no longer had meaning for him unless he could find some way of reconciling the science he practiced with the spiritual world in which he believed. After a dozen years as a reclusive invalid, he suddenly recovered.

> The primary result of [the crisis] was a deepening of Fechner's religious consciousness and his interest in the problem of the soul. . . . his philosophical solution of the spiritual problem lay in his affirmation of the identity of mind and matter and in his assurance that the entire universe can be regarded as readily from the point of view of its consciousness (Boring, 1950, 278).

Fechner felt that if the mind and body were two manifestations of a single consciousness (i.e, Parmenides' One), then there should be physical constants that reflected the connection between the two. He wanted to find some way to actually quantify physical relationships between the mental and physical realms. Fechner found just such quantification in the work of Ernst Heinrich Weber. Weber conducted a series of experiments in which he tried to discover the threshold of sensory awareness. He had a subject hold a weight, then a second weight which was slightly heavier. He kept increasing the difference between the weights until the subject could detect a difference. He found that "the smallest perceptible difference between two weights can be stated as a ratio between the weights, a ratio that is independent of the magnitudes of the weights" (Heidbreder, 1933, 81; Boring, 1950, 113).

Not only that, but the ratio was constant for all subjects, and moreover, the results were similar in his experiments with visual and auditory response. That may sound commonplace. After all, it merely says that the heavier the weight, the larger the difference between it and the second weight before any difference can be detected. *This means, however, that the sensory world is experienced through relationship, not through absolute difference. But if there was no intermediate third between the world and the mind, then our experience should be absolute, not relative.*

To Fechner, Weber's experiments were a revelation, and he called the results Weber's Law. Actually, it might better be called Fechner's Law since Weber never saw the full significance of his discoveries, nor did he develop the general form of the law. As Fechner stated Weber's Law, sensation (which Fechner felt to be a purely mental process) varied with the natural logarithm of the stimulus (which Fechner felt was purely physical). Another way of expressing Weber's Law is that response varies arithmetically as stimulus varies geometrically. Fechner spent the next decade extending that research, to which he gave the name *psychophysics*.

A hundred years later, S. S. Stevens vastly extended Weber's and Fechner's research on psychophysics. As with most pioneering results, Weber's initial guess was overly crude. Stevens showed that the ratio between sensation and stimulus was a *power function,* not merely a logarithmic function; i.e., the sensation equaled some constant that varied with the particular kind of sensation being measured, times the measurement of the stimulus to some power (often fractional). Though this modified Weber's Law, it further proved that the relationship between sensation and stimulus is relational, not direct. (Stevens, 1951, 1958).

EARLY 20TH CENTURY

Behavioral vs. Gestalt Psychology

Early in the twentieth-century, John B. Watson developed a stimulus-response model that became behaviorism. All behavior is considered to be composed of s-r chains, where a stimulus leads to a response, which in turn becomes the stimulus for still another response. Both stimulus and response are purely physiological events, and hence fully measurable. The mind in between can be safely ignored as, at most, an epiphenomenon.

Behaviorism fit both the climate of the time and the American character. Though never influential in Europe, it quickly became the dominant branch of American psychology. At roughly the same time that Watson was developing his s-r model, German psychologists explored Gestalt psychology. Gestalt is a difficult word to translate but roughly means the total context. Gestalt psychologists argued that perception, for example, could never be understood by simple chains of associations or stimulus response units. In a series of classic experiments, independently conducted by German Gestalt psychologist Wolfgang Kohler and American neuropsychologist Karl Lashley, chickens were taught to distinguish two different shades of gray; we'll call them Gray and Dark-Gray. If the chickens correctly identified Dark-Gray, they received a reward of food. With the chickens trained to pick Dark-Gray, the psychologists brought in a still darker gray, which we'll call Gray-Black. They exposed the chickens to Dark-Gray and Gray-Black.

Now, if behaviorism was correct, the chickens should once more have picked Dark-Gray, because they had supposedly made a straightforward association of Dark-Gray with a reward of food. In fact, a small percentage of chickens did just that. But the overwhelming majority of chickens picked Gray-Black, the darker shade. In other words, most chickens had associated a relationship, "darker", with getting a reward (Kohler, 1947,118).

It is important to stress that the chickens were not exposed to a series of situations in which they had to pick the darker shade of gray. They were only trained with the one pair of grays, yet most learned from that one situation to pick the darker shade. In these experiments, stimuli did not lead immediately to response; "between the stimulus and the response, there occurs the process of organization" (Kohler, 1947, 119). Thus, even at the sensory level, experience is structured relationally. These experiments were extended to apes (thus much closer to humans), and to the perception of size (where the relationship of smaller to larger proved more primary than the actual size of an object.)

These, and many similar experiments, show that not only humans, but animals also organize sensory perception. The question of how much organization goes on at various levels between the original sensory perception and the eventual complex organization in the psyche is an open question. But clearly "The organizing principles of experiential realities are to be found in logical realities;" where logic is used in the broadest sense of some organizational model, some algorithm. The discovery that relatively simply algorithms can organize complex structures and actions is, of course, central in dynamics.

Platonic Ideals Become Jungian Archetypes

At much the same time as both behaviorism and Gestalt psychology were emerging, a third voice appeared from a new direction: depth psychology. Though it was

Sigmund Freud who brought depth psychology into being, we are more concerned here with Freud's younger colleague: Carl Gustav Jung. Early in their association, Freud anointed Jung as his successor, only to then excommunicate him when Jung's views took directions antithetical to Freud's. While working as a young doctor at the Burgholzli Mental Clinic in Switzerland, Jung conducted word association experiments where he not only recorded the patient's response to a stimulus word, but also measured the reaction time of the response. Interestingly, he found that the responses with the longest reaction times tended to cluster around subjects that had emotional significance for the patient. In other words, Jung had discovered once again that there was a "missing third" between action and reaction.

For the first time, however, these intervening organizational entities were associated with emotional subject matter which could be classified into groupings which he called "complexes;" i.e., a whole array of stimulus words might have similar delays in reaction time. When he studied those stimulus words and tried to discover what, if anything, they might have in common for that particular patient, he found that they tended to group around single issues; mother issues, for example. Further, he found that the same emotional clusters (again we'll say mother issues, though there are many such complexes) occurred in other patients as well. What could form such a core? Why did it have such energy? Jung used the term *archetype* (from the Greek for "prime imprinter") for the core of a complex. In our example, a mother archetype would then be posited as lying at the center of a mother complex. Jung simply argued that "psychological existence is subjective in so far as an idea occurs in only one individual. But it is objective in so far as that idea is shared by a society--by a *consensus gentium*" (Jung, 1969, p. 6).

Archetypes, like Plato's ideas, were ideal forms; they didn't, however, exist in some idealized world, but instead both in the inner world of the mind and the structure of physical reality. Jung's theory subsumed both of our earlier suppositions, that: (1) the organizing principles of experiential realities are to be found in logical realities, and (2) the organizing principles of logical realities are to be found in first principles outside of those realities.

Jung liked to compare an archetype to a river bed which has been slowly formed over thousands of years. Originally there was just a stream of water which followed the path of least resistance on its way to the sea. The water followed any of a number of different branches, one as likely as the next. However, as time slowly passed, it became less and less likely that the water would take any path other than those already traced many times previously.

However, if circumstances changed drastically enough, a new path could still form. For example, if a rockfall dammed up a portion of the river, the water would be forced to take a new direction. If it eventually branched back into the old path, at least it would have taken a new route for part of the journey. But perhaps part of the river never made it back to the old bed and a new tributary formed. Similarly the emergence of a new archetype.

2ND HALF OF THE 20TH CENTURY

Ethology: Lorenz & the Imprinting Process

In the latter half of the 20th century, science started to find proof for something quite like Jung's concept of archetypes, though neither Jung nor archetypes were ever mentioned. Following Watson & Crick's dramatic discovery of the structure of DNA in 1953, molecular biology began to make astonishing advances in demonstrating how the person we is stored in our DNA. But of more interest for our discussion were the discoveries in ethology, which carefully traced how, in the animal kingdom, inherited behaviors stored in the brain are triggered by environmental cues. As with so many areas of thought in psychology, psychologist William James already realized that the brain exists as part of the world, and must necessarily be adapted to it.

> *Mental facts cannot properly be studied apart from the physical environment of which they take cognizance* . . . our inner faculties are *adapted* in advance to the features of the world in which we dwell. . . . Mind and world in short have evolved together, and in consequence are something of a mutual fit (Anderson & Rosenfeld, 1988, 1).

The brain preserves its evolutionary history in its structure. It has stored an immense number of behaviors that have proved useful for our ancestors in the human and animal world over vast periods of time. Certain situations repeat over and over for every member of a species. Frogs have to be very good at recognizing flies or they will go hungry. Humans have to be very good at recognizing human faces or they can't function within any human social structure. So there has to be a great deal of specificity in what is stored in the brain (Anderson & Rosenfeld, 1988, 2). On the other hand, every creature is in large part born into a world unique to it, and has to be able to adapt to that world.

For example, though all creatures are born from a mother and, in a majority of species, are raised by the mother, mothers come in a great variety of different packages. Nature has to handle both the specificity and the variety. For example, in his *King Solomon's Ring* (1952, 47), Nobel prize winning ethologist Konrad Lorenz explains that "greylag goslings unquestioningly accept the first living being whom they meet as their mother." But with mallards, he found that it wasn't enough to be the first person they saw at birth; in addition, he "must quack like a mother mallard in order to make the little ducks run after me" (Lorenz, 1952, 48). That turned out to do the trick. Though he looked about as much like a mother mallard "as Calvin Coolidge looks like Metro Goldwyn Mayer's lion" (as James Thurber so perfectly described the wolf masquerading as Red Riding Hood's grandmother in his *Fables for our Time*), simply making the proper quacking sound was enough to convince the little ducks that Lorenz was their mother.

The mother's response is as instinctive as the baby's; more recent research has shown this extends to humans as well as other animals. Nor are such inherited behaviors limited to mother/child behavior. Courting rituals are also instinctive in most species. An adult male jackdaw fell in love with Lorenz and tried all the wiles that normally proved successful with female jackdaws. For example, he kept trying to feed Lorenz delicacies like ground-up worms. Like a true scientist, Lorenz suffered this disgusting diet as long as he could. When he was finally so sick of the taste of worms that he refused to open his mouth, the jackdaw filled his ear with worms, then was disappointed when this proved a less than successful romantic strategy (Lorenz, 1952, 153-4).

A baby's recognition of mother, an adult's repertoire of courting behavior, both innate. Recognition of danger is also often inborn. "Magpies, mallards or robins, prepare at once for flight at their very first sight of a cat, a fox or even a squirrel." It made no difference whether they were raised by humans or by birds. In contrast, jackdaws, who we have seen are born knowing so much about love, have to be taught to recognize danger by their parents. Though they may not be born with a sense of self-preservation, they are, however, born with a innate need to protect their young at all costs. Since jackdaws--including baby jackdaws--are black, "any living being that carries a black thing, dangling or fluttering, becomes the object of furious onslaught." Poor Lorenz discovered this to his distress when he accidentally picked up a baby jackdaw and was instantly attacked by the mother. He dropped the baby, and was left with a wounded and bloody hand. Now forewarned, Lorenz systematically explored just how far this instinctual behavior extended. He found, for example, that he could safely carry his black camera, but "the jackdaws would start their rattling cry as soon as I pulled out the black paper strips of the pack film which fluttered to and fro in the breeze" (all quotes Lorenz, 1952, 157-9). This happened even though the adult birds knew Lorenz to be their friend and no threat to their children. Instinct simply took over.

Though we have a considerably greater ability to take conscious control of our actions than a jackdaw, a huge amount of our behaviors are already stored away at birth in our brains, ready to be triggered into action when needed. The missing 3rd not only resides in the brain, but it is pre adapted because it and its environment evolved together. But we still need one further piece to our puzzle: a model for the dynamic relationship of brain, mind, and world.

Cybernetics: McCulloch-Pitts vs. Gregory Bateson

When [Norbert] Wiener brought the feedback idea to the foreground, not only did it become immediately recognized as a fundamental concept, but it also raised major philosophical questions as to the validity of the cause-effect doctrine. . . . the nature of feedback is that it gives a mechanism, which is independent of particular properties, of components, for constituting a stable unit. And from this mechanism, the appearance of stability gives a rationale to the observed purposive behavior of systems and a possibility of understanding teleology (Varela, 1979, 166-167).

Before nonlinear dynamics, there was general systems theory. And before general systems theory, there was cybernetics. Cybernetics first emerged from the fertile mind of Norbert Wiener (1948/1961), with a healthy dose of John von Neumann tossed into the mix. But it was really the Macy Conferences--a series of 10 interdisciplinary conferences beginning in 1946 and continuing through 1953--that took cybernetics from the idea stage to a fully-developed field. [In this section on the Macy conferences, I'm largely drawing on (Heims, 1991)].

Throughout the annual conferences of the Society for Chaos Theory in Psychology, there has always been a creative tension between two complementary (and sometimes opposing) groups, which I usually characterize in my mind as the "techies" and the "metaphorists." The Macy conferences had their equivalent split between what historian Steve Heims calls the "cyberneticians" and the "social scientists". During WWII, social science had moved out of the college classroom and beyond theory into application, due to the need for psychologists, anthropologists, and sociologists in the war effort. The Macy conferences marked the first time when hard science and soft science came together to discuss a single idea, each trying to offer its own unique perspective.

What was so important about cybernetics that it could unite such a varied group, much as chaos theory would later unite a similarly broad spectrum of disciplines?

> First, it was concerned with goal-directed actions, where an organism acts with a purpose. . . . Second, the model replaced the traditional cause-and-effect

relation of a stimulus leading to a response by a "circular causality" requiring negative feedback (Heims, 1991, 15).

Previously science had relegated ideas of goal-directedness--teleology--to the scrapheap of pre-scientific notions like vitalism or spontaneous generation. Cause-and-effect, building ineluctably from past causes to future effects, could explain all. Cybernetics supplied a new way of viewing reality that lent itself to scientific description and even mechanical realization, yet could deal with situations too complex for simple causality to explain. At its simplest level, imagine a thermostat regulating air conditioning. The thermostat will continuously compare the actual temperature--let's say it's 75 degrees--with whatever desired temperature you have set the thermostat at--70 degrees in this example. As long as the actual temperature is warmer than the desired temperature, the air conditioning will come on and stay on. When the actual temperature reaches 70 degrees, the thermostat will shut off the air-conditioning. It will stay off until the temperature once more climbs above the desired setting. And this will be done in a mechanical manner which doesn't involve itself with philosophical issues like teleology.

Even our little thermostat already involves both the key concepts in cybernetics: positive and negative feedback. Positive: keep doing what you're doing;

negative: hey, stop already. Seen in that light, cybernetics hardly seems startling, but it was a major break from Newtonian dynamics.

Let's take two contrasting examples of the attendees of the Macy conferences, one each from the "cyberneticians" and one from the "social scientists." Representing the cyberneticians, psychiatrist and research physiologist Warren McCulloch combined with boy genius (well, almost a boy, as he was only 20 at the time) Walter Pitts to create the McCulloch-Pitts theorem for neural nets. This was the first "computer" model of the brain; what was truly remarkable is that the concept preceded actual computers. All references in McCulloch's and Pitts' original paper were to mathematical logic. They viewed the neuron as an binary device which could receive either excitatory or inhibitory inputs from the synapses. When the value of these inputs passes a certain threshold, the neuron turns on or off. If enough of these simplified neurons are linked together into a closed network, McCulloch and Pitts proved that a large class of logical problems can be solved. Essentially, they presented the brain as a Universal Turing Device, or what we now call a computer (McCulloch and Pitts, 1943). Of course, we now know that the neuron and the linkage between neurons, is much more complex than this, more organic, less mechanical. Still this was a brilliant starting point.

In his youth, after studying Bertrand Russell's then seminal work in which mathematics was viewed as a subset of logic, McCulloch was tantalized by the deep philosophical question "what is a man that he can know a number?" Attempting to answer that question led him into first psychology, then neurophysiology, but it was the power of logic that drove him. Pitts was an autodidact who "was known to master the contents of a textbook in a field new to him in a few days." Even gifted scientists would defer to him for a logical analysis of any issue within their own fields. McCulloch was for a good while a father figure for Pitts (as was also, to a lesser extent, Norbert Wiener). Together McCulloch and Pitts made an impressive single representative for the power of logic.

Anthropologist Gregory Bateson was an equally impressive spokesman for the other camp. He grew up in a highly intellectual British family. His father was a "major, albeit controversial, figure within British biology" who championed the rediscovery of Mendel's work. Growing up with biological issues in his bones, he initially chose zoology as a field, then moved on to anthropology, to which he brought an ecological point of view long before ecology existed as a field. In Heims' book on the group, he characterizes Bateson as a "scout" not only for the Macy group, but throughout his career. "From anthropology and learning theory he moved to psychiatry, behavior of otters and octopus, theory of humor, kinesics, language and learning among dolphins, and theory of evolution" (Heims, 1991, 251).

At the Macy conferences Bateson often presented anthropological examples of cybernetic feedback mechanisms in various cultures, "including the case of the Iatmul culture in which a transvestite ceremony served as a homeostatic mechanism whenever a characteristic patten of aggressive actions within the tribe threatened to divide them" (Heims, 1991, Bateson, 1958).

That must seem like pretty small stuff in comparison with the McCulloch-Pitts model which led to neural nets. But Bateson's ability to cut across academic disciplines allowed him to scout out new areas of thought, to sniff out what was important, to ask the central questions before anyone else even knew there was anything to be asked. Of course, like all scouts, once a new field--like cybernetics--achieved respectability, his questions were unfortunately often dismissed as irrelevant by those more intent on the matters at hand. We are only now coming to reexamine questions Bateson raised half a century ago. For example, in his own work, he distinguished learning from "learning to learn" ("proto-learning" and "deutero-learning" respectively). Applying that to computers, Bateson asked the group "whether computers can learn to learn, and how in a formal mathematical way one could distinguish that from plain learning" (Heims, 1991, 24, also see Wiener, 1950/54).

Through the decade of the conference, and beyond them until his death in 1980, Bateson continued to extend the scope of these cybernetic questions. In 1968, fifteen years after the last Macy conference, he organized a conference on the "Effects of Conscious Purpose on Human Adaption." As an introduction, he offered 11 "considerations." The first seven discuss cybernetic systems in general. The last four move into the relationship between mind and world. I'm going to paraphrase 8 and 9, and quote Bateson directly on the last two:

> 8. The contents of consciousness have to be selected somehow from a huge set of possibilities within the mind. We know little or nothing about how this is accomplished.
> 9. Those contents appear to be "importantly related to 'purpose,' 'attention,' and similar phenomena," about which we also know very little.
> 10. "If consciousness has feedback upon the remainder of mind and if consciousness deals only with a skewed sample of the events of the total mind, then there must exist a systemic (i.e., non-random) difference between the conscious views of self and the world and the true nature of self and the world. Such a difference must distort the processes of adaption."

11. "It is suggested that the specific nature of this distortion is such that the *cybernetic nature of self and the world tends to be imperceptible to consciousness*" (Bateson, M., 1972, 16).

As we see, the question of the missing 3rd now has moved forward into the nature of consciousness itself and its emergence from the "cybernetic nature of self and world." Cyberneticians, most prominently Heinz von Foerster, then began to examine what is now termed "second-order cybernetics", the cybernetics that includes the consciousness of the observer in the cybernetics process. Umberto Maturana and Francisco Varela extended cybernetic concepts deeply into biology and developed *autopoeisis,* the idea that sufficiently complex biological systems (such as individual animals and human beings) continually feed information about their identity back into themselves in order to preserve their identity in time despite widely varying conditions.

But there was still another field emerging that had something to add to this dialogue: chaos theory.

Chaos Theory

Though Chaos Theory has led to a wide variety of new understandings about nature, perhaps most famously, three discoveries stand out: 1) small changes can lead to large effects; 2) determinism and predictability are not synonymous in any sufficiently complex system that involves feedback; and 3) in far from equilibrium systems, order can emerge from within. It is the third of these discoveries that best applies to our discussion of the missing third, most specifically with "attractors." In his book, *Society of Brains* (1995), neuro-scientist Walter Freeman describes the discovery of sensory "attractors" in the brain:

> This book had its origin in an experimental finding and an insight. First, the finding. I was tracing the path taken by neural activity that accompanies and followed a sensory stimulus in brains of rabbits. I traced it from the sensory receptors into the cerebral cortex and there found that the activity vanished, just like the rabbit down the rabbit hole in "Alice in Wonderland." What appeared in place of the stimulus-evoked activity was a new pattern of cortical activity that was created by the rabbit brain. (p. 2).

Freeman and his students found that this discovery ranged across all the sensory systems: sight, sound, smell, feel. In all cases, once the stimuli hit the brain, they disappeared, and instead information previously stored in the brain appeared. And that information could be triggered by different sensory stimuli. He concluded, like Kant, that his rabbit could never have any knowledge of "das ding an sich," the actual world; it only knew the world of its brain. Clearly the brain seems to contain "attractors" which are similar to Kant's categories, Jung's archetypes. The ethological evidence seems conclusive on this point. But there is also the possibility that "attractors" can come into existence in real time and then function much like inherited categories or archetypes thereafter.

The first discovery of chaos theory, small changes can have large effects, comes into play here. Physical order can remain over a wide variety of circumstances, but then some small change, and this change can be internal to the system, not necessarily imposed from without, can lead to a total change of order, through the path of bifurcations leading to chaos, then to new order. The second discovery, that new order can emerge from within when there is feedback, shows why this can happen. Of course, this doesn't mean that we understand "emergence." It's a new mystery to which we have only given a name.

But we see examples of this actually happening in both mathematics and nature. In mathematics, both the logistics map and the Mandelbrot set, provide elegant examples. In the logistics map, very simple equation, coupled with feedback, can lead from order to chaos to new order. In the Mandelbrot set, we see again a simple equation, coupled with feedback, leading either to chaos or to self-similar order. In chemistry, the Belousov-

Zhabotinsky reaction provides a lovely example of emergent self-similar order.

Neural nets also provide examples of how new attractors can emerge. For example, neuro-scientist Gary Lynch collaborated with computer scientist Richard Granger in developing a computer model of a 500 neuron network to see if it could learn to discriminate between different smells. They had two different smell groups: "cheese" and "flower," with variations of each. At first the neural net came up with a unique pattern for each smell, but eventually, after it was exposed to the individual odors more times, the neural net produced one pattern for the cheeses and another for the flowers. Without any instruction or any logic, it was able to generalize from the specific examples to the group to which they belonged. If they exposed it to any of the "cheese" smells, for example, it would always identify "cheese."

But something even more startling happened: as they continued to give it more sniffs of each particular cheese, at some point, the general pattern disappeared and the neural net then produced specific patterns for the various cheeses, within the general pattern. Now the network could not only discriminate "cheeses" from "flowers," but also different varieties of "cheeses." Granger said that:

> We're thrilled with it. With the first sniff, it recognizes the overall pattern and says, "it's a cheese." With the

next sniffs, it distinguishes the pattern and says, "It's Jarlsberg" (Allman, 1989, p. 76).

So chaos theory advances our problem of the missing third still further. Now we can see examples of how form can emerge from chaos without any order imposed being from without. There is no longer necessarily a contradiction between Parmenides "One" and Plato's "Ideas," since the Ideas can emerge from within the One spontaneously. The missing third becomes the chaos that intervenes between one order and the next.

Summary

We began this essay with Socrates' assertion that the qualities we attach to the things of the world are merely copies of copies of idealized forms that exist outside the world. Parmenides argued that any such idealized quality could then be included among the things to which it applied, and there would then necessarily be a *third*, a quality which described all both worldly objects and the Platonic ideal. This would then lead into an infinite regress. The problem, he argued, is because the world is an undifferentiated whole, a *One*, which includes both ideal and actual.

The Neoplatonists of the 3rd to 5th century, resolved this problem by positing a graduated hierarchy between highest and lowest rather than a continuum, with each stage composed of emanations from the One. In its most developed form, expressed by Proclus, each stage was holographic, since it contained the possibility of immediate apprehension of the One.

With the emergence of science in the seventeenth century, Locke proposed a new model in which the mind was a *tabula rasa,* a blank slate, at birth. All ideas contained in the mind were either records of sensations, or of combinations of sensations. At much the same time, Descartes asserted *cogito, ergo, sum* (I think, therefore I am), which asserted that the proper starting point for examination of the world was our thoughts.

In the eighteenth century, Berkeley took Descartes starting point to its logical conclusion and denied the reality of the outside world since all we know are our thoughts. Late in the century, Kant took the biggest step forward since Plato and resolved the paradox by asserting that the mind contains inherent categories which organize our sensory perceptions of physical reality. Hence there was a missing third already existent in the mind.

In the nineteenth century, Fechner fleshed out Weber's experimental results on the perception of weight differences to demonstrate that there was an intermediate organization that lay between physical stimuli and our sensory awareness of this stimuli.

In the early twentieth century, Watson developed behaviorism, which denied the need for mind, and simply viewed behavior as composed of series of stimulus-response chains. Hence no missing third. But Kohler, Lashley and other Gestalt psychologists demonstrated clearly that Fechner was correct that sensory perception was relational, not direct. Jung then took the final step with his model of archetypes which provided a model of the structure of the missing third that lies between the mind and the world.

Later in the twentieth century, ethology provided details for just how archetypes are stored in the brain and triggered by environmental cues at necessary points of development. Cybernetics demonstrated that mind, brain, and world are tied together in a loop in which each informs the other. This leads to the emergence of consciousness, a consciousness unaware of this cybernetic relationship. Finally, late in the twentieth century, chaos theory showed how new form could emerge from within spontaneously in systems complex enough to contain feedback.

We think of science as progressive, with old questions dying as new answers emerge. But eternal questions are never fully answered. Instead, they are recast within the intellectual climate of an era, usually without any awareness that the same question had occurred time and again in the past. The case of the missing third is just such an eternal question. We can only wonder what new form it will take in the future? Personally I think it may come from paying more attention to unresolved issues such as those posed by Gregory Bateson thirty-five years ago. Or perhaps looking more deeply at how emergent attractors overlap with stored archetypes, as posited by Jung a hundred years ago. Or perhaps even by turning all the way back to Plato and Parmenides and realizing that, in some ways, their argument is as new and unanswered today at it was two and a half millennia ago.

REFERENCES

Anderson, James and Rosenfeld, Edward (eds.) *Neurocomputing: Foundations of Research*. Cambridge: MIT Press, 1988.

Bateson, Gregory. *Naven, 6th edition,* (Stanford: Stanford University Press, 1958).

Bateson, Mary Catherine. *Our Own Metaphor* (New York: Alfred A. Knopf, 1972).

Boring, Edwin G. *A History of Experimental Psychology,* 2nd ed. (New York: Appleton-Century-Crofts, 1950).

Cornford, Francis M. (Trans.) *Plato and Parmenides,* (New York: The Liberal Arts Press, 1957).
Excerpt from the World Wide Web:
http://faculty.washington.edu/smcohen/parm132.html.

*Freeman, Walter J.*Societies of Brains: A Study in the Neuroscience of Love and Hate. *(Hillsdale, NJ: Erlbaum, 1995).*

Gillispie, Charles D. *Dictionary of Scientific Biography.* (New York: MacMillan, 1980). Excerpt from the World Wide Web: http://www-gap.dcs.st-and.ac.uk/~history/Mathematicians /Zeno_of_Elea.html.

Gregson, R. "Herbart and 'Psychological Research on the Strength of a Given Impression.'" *Nonlinear Dynamics, Psychology, and Life Sciences,* vol. 2, no. 3. (New York: Human Sciences Press, 1985).

Heath, Sir Thomas. A History of Greek mathematics: From Thales to Euclid. *(Dover, 1981).*

Heidbreder, Edna. *Seven Psychologies.* (New York: Appleton-Century-Crofts. 1933).

Heims, Steve. *The Cybernetics Group.* (Cambridge, Mass.: MIT Press, 1991).

James, William.*The Principles of Psychology, vol.1.* 2 volume reprint of 1st ed. of 1890. (New York: Dover Publications, 1950).

Jung, C. G. *Collected Works, Vol. 8: The Structure and Dynamics of the Psyche.* (Princeton: Bollingen Series, Princeton University Press, 1960).

Jung, C. G. *Collected Works, Vol. 3: Symbols of Transformation, 2nd ed.* (Princeton: Bollingen Series, Princeton University Press, 1867).

Jung, C. G. *Collected Works, Vol. 11: Psychology and Religion: West and East, 2nd ed.* (Princeton: Bollingen Series, Princeton University Pres, 1969).

Kohler, Wolfgang. *Gestalt Psychology.* (New York: Mentor Books, New American Library, 1947).

Lorenz, Konrad. *King Solomon's Ring.* (New York: Time Incorporated, 1952).

McCulloch, W. and Pitts, W. "A logical calculus of the ideas immanent in nervous activity", *Bulletin of Mathematical Biophysics* 5: 115-133. 1943).

Reese, William L. *Dictionary of Philosophy and Religion.* (New Jersey: Humanities Press, 1980).

Stevens, Stanley S. *Handbook of Experimental Psychology*. (New York: Wiley, 1951).

Stevens, Stanley S. "Problems and Methods of Psychophysics", *Psychological Bulletin, 55,* 1958.

Varela, Francisco. *Principles of Biological Autonomy.* (New York: North Holland,1979).

Wiener, Norbert. The Human Use of Human Beings: Cybernetics and Society, revised edition *(New York: De Capo Press, 1950/54).*

Wiener, Norbert. *Cybernetics, 2nd edition.* (Cambridge, Mass.: MIT Press, 1948/1961).

Whitehead, Alfred North. *Process and Reality,* Corrected Edition. David Ray Griffin and Donald W. Sherburne, Eds. (New York: The Free Press, 1929/1978).

SCINTILLAE OF LIGHT

CHAOS AND EMERGENCE

There is, in my opinion, no tenable argument against the hypothesis that all the psychic functions which today seem conscious to us were once unconscious and yet worked as if they were *conscious.*

- C. G. Jung. [1]

How is it that consciousness emerges? One answer to that deep question comes from Western alchemy, whose study was to occupy Jung for so many years. Because the alchemists were projecting their inner struggle out onto their experiments, Jung could find the stages of the individuation process prefigured within the alchemical operations. In particular the manner in which consciousness emerged from the chaos of the unconscious. "The alchemists understood the return to chaos as an essential part of the opus." [2] Chaos by its very nature has yet no structure, yet because of this it potentially contains all structure. At some point, the alchemists saw little points of light appear in the darkness. They would appear, then disappear back into the darkness, the chaos. At some unpredictable point, one point no longer disappeared; it would become brighter until it achieved a permanency. Jung interpreted this as the emergence of consciousness (more on all this later).

This model of the dynamics of emergence is now finding new support from the unexpected area of chaos/complexity theory (more broadly "non-linear dynamics"). In chaos theory, once order has disintegrated into chaos (through a precisely determined progression), little points of order begin to emerge. Eventually, at some unpredictable point, one of those points becomes a center around which other points gather until a new order begins to emerge. For example, picture a pan of water as it begins to reaching the boiling point. Whirls of heat appear here and there, then disappear back into the water. If one watches closely, at the point when the water begins to fully boil, the whirls gather together around one central point. Then the water changes state, to steam. A new order has emerged.

This paper explores what this unusual pairing has to teach us. We have to examine both alchemy and chaos theory in order to see how they both come together in Jungian psychology. Let us begin with a short history of alchemy.

A SHORT HISTORY OF ALCHEMY (3)

We are probably justified in assuming that alchemy deals with the same or very similar processes as those involved in active imagination and in dreams, i.e., ultimately with the process of individuation.

- C. G. Jung. (4)

Alchemy has generally been presented as a foolish, superstitious predecessor to chemistry. Most of us know little or nothing of the actual practice of alchemy. Perhaps we visualize solitary men working with beakers and flasks--that portrait would be partially accurate. We might be aware that the goal of alchemy was the production of the *philosopher's stone,* but we have little idea what that might be. We might also vaguely remember that alchemists attempted--and sometimes claimed to have succeeded in--the transmutation of lead into gold. This gives us a picture of the alchemist as either a greedy fool or a charlatan. Though alchemists included both fools and charlatans among their number, as have every other calling, most alchemists were neither. They were likely to be intelligent, religious, inquisitive, and necessarily solitary. In order to understand how alchemy could possibly offer anything of substance for depth psychology, we have to understand a little of the history of alchemy.

Alchemy and Christianity came into existence in the Western world at roughly the same time. Alchemy developed into a separate field during the 1st through the 3rd century. However, its roots can be traced to 330 B.C., when Alexander the Great conquered Egypt, founded the city of Alexandria, and created the greatest library of the ancient world. The library, which housed nearly half a million manuscripts, brought scholars from all over the world. Even though a great part of the library burned during Caesar's conquest of Alexandria in 80 B.C., it remained a haven for scholars. During this period, commerce, warfare and Christianity all served to mix cultures that had hitherto gone their separate ways. John Stillman, in his history of alchemy and early chemistry, says of these times that "Greek philosophy, Egyptian arts, Chaldean and Persian mysticism met and gave rise to strange combinations not always conducive to improvement upon the relative clarity of the Greek foundation." (5) Obviously, Stillman shares the views of alchemy as a naive pre-science that I've mentioned earlier. His views are typical of the histories of alchemy written from the viewpoint of Western science. In contrast, Jungian analyst Marie-Louise von Franz saw alchemy as an advance which combined Greek theory with Egyptian experimentation.

> The Greek philosophers who, as you all know, initiated rational thought regarding the problems of nature, of matter, space and time, etc., made practically no or very few experiments. Their theories

are bolstered by certain observations but it never really occurred to them to actually experiment. On the other hand, in Egypt there was a highly developed chemical-magical technique, but in general the Egyptians gave it no thought, either philosophical or theoretical. It was simply the handing down by certain priestly orders of practical recipes, plus some magic religious representation but I should say without theoretical reflection. When the two trends of Greek and Egyptian civilization came together they united in a very fruitful marriage, of which alchemy was their child. (6)

The first great alchemists were also Gnostic Christians. Christianity was, in these early days, largely the religion of the simpler, less-educated members of society. The Gnostics tended to be more intellectual; they viewed Christianity as the newest and greatest of the *mystery religions,* in which deep truths were hidden beneath the innocent words preached to the masses. Gnostics wanted a personal experience of God, not merely a collective religion interpreted for them by priests. Because of this need for personal experience, they developed a complex symbolic system to describe the relationship between God, humanity, and the world. (7) Of course, as Jung said: "it seems highly unlikely that they had a psychological conception of [their symbolic images]." (8)

Since Jung's time, much more material has come to light on the wide variety of views lumped under the title of Gnostic. Christianity was just beginning to solidify into the form it would hold for so many centuries, while those with divergent views were united more by their opposition to the ruling ideas than any unity of beliefs. That being said, there is still much to be said for the view of Gnostics as ancient precursors of modern men and women on a spiritual quest.

The alchemists were trying to discover the deepest secrets of the universe. For them, that meant searching for the building blocks of both matter and psyche, for they saw no clear distinction between the two: there was only the relationship between the experimenter and his experiment. An alchemical operation had to be conducted at a propitious time because they believed that the micro world of their experiments was connected with the macro world of the cosmos. They had to meditate deeply on both their own inner nature and the inner nature of the matter upon which they were experimenting. It is easy to see why this seemed to Jung a prefiguration of modern depth psychology, in which the psychologist must observe not only their patients' psyches, but their own as well, since the two are inextricably connected in the process of therapy.

After the 3rd century, the alchemical tradition (along with mathematics and other deep mysteries) spread to the Moslem world. There existed in Islam, as in

Christianity, a split between the outer-oriented religion of the masses, and a more inner-oriented, mystical religion followed by the intellectuals. The latter eagerly adopted alchemy as one more avenue into the greater mysteries. With the Arab conquest of Spain during the 7th and 8th centuries, Arabian alchemy moved back into the Western world. There the mystery teachings spread to the Jewish mystics, with the Cabala as the major product. During the 12th and 13th centuries, these ideas spread beyond Spain to the rest of Western Europe. By the late 13th century, Europeans were writing their own alchemical texts, most notably Albertus Magnus, Roger Bacon, and Raymond Lull.

In his rich book *Alchemy,* Johannes Fabricius comments on the position of the alchemists:

> Because the alchemists originated in a pre-Christian cultural world, they had to establish themselves as a subculture in medieval Christianity. Here they occupied a strange position, religiously as well as scientifically. The alchemists were mystics without being orthodox Catholics, scientists without following the learning of their time, artisans unwilling to teach others what they knew. They were sectarians, the problem-children of medieval society, and their contemporaries were ever hesitant about deciding whether to regard them as pure sages or sacrilegious impostors. (9)

Western alchemy reached its peak in the 15th and 16th centuries and still existed in some form during the 17th and 18th centuries. For example, Isaac Newton, who changed the world forever with his scientific discoveries in the 17th century, was a practicing alchemist who regarded his alchemical studies as of equal or greater importance with his scientific studies. In his alchemical notes, he commented that "just as the world was created from dark Chaos through the bringing forth of light, so our work brings forth the beginning out of black chaos and its first matter." (10) Note again the reference to "bringing forth of light . . . out of the black chaos." Newton saw no discrepancy between the two positions of alchemist and scientist. Whereas the world he presented for science was a world of absolutes, he saw the deeper world revealed by alchemy as perpetually changing, transforming: "For nature is a perpetuall circulatory worker, generating fluids out of solids, and solids out of liquids, fixed things out of volatile, & volatile out of fixes, subtile out of gross, & gross out of subtile." Thus Newton stood at a pivotal point between the two world-views. We need to follow the winding trail that led from Newton to a science that ignored the older traditions, but eventually culminated in chaos theory. Here, as so often in the history of thought, we encounter "old wine in new bottles."

THE CLOCKWORK UNIVERSE OF ISAAC NEWTON

"Nature and nature's laws lay hid in night, God said Let Newton be! and all was light."

- poet Alexander Pope, in his epitaph for Newton. [(11)]

It is hard to over-estimate the impact of Isaac Newton's discoveries on the Western World. With his *Optiks* and *Principia,* Newton seemed to his contemporaries to have explained all of nature: motion, force, gravity, and light. Before Newton, there were speculations; after Newton there were Laws! Newton's scientific world was a world of absolutes: absolute space and time, and perfect, indivisible particles moving in that absolute space and time. In Newton's words from his masterwork, the *Principia*: "Absolute space, in its own nature, without relation to anything external remains always similar and immovable. Absolute, true, and mathematical time, in itself, and from its own nature, flows equably without relation to anything external." [(12)]

Both space and time were subsumed within his laws. It was this world-view of fixed laws that seemingly described all of reality, that inspired the next generation of scientists. Newtonian physics was used to support the deistic view that God had created the world as a perfect machine that then required no further interference from Him. The world was like a clock that had been created, wound up, then set in place. It was up to humanity to discover first, how the clock was built, then the laws on which it ran. These ideals were typified in 18th century mathematician and astronomer Pierre Simon Laplace's expressed view that a Supreme Intelligence, armed with a knowledge of Newtonian laws of nature and a knowledge of the positions and velocities of all particles in the Universe at any moment, could deduce the state of the Universe at any time past or present. "All the effects of nature are only the mathematical consequences of a small number of immutable laws." (13)

Laplace's masterpiece was the *Mecanique Celeste,* which took on the formidable task of fully explaining the movements of the planets, their effects on the tides, and much more. There is a famous anecdote concerning Napoleon's reaction to the book. Napoleon told Laplace: "You have written this huge book on the system of the world without once mentioning the author of the universe." Laplace answered: "Sire, I had no need of that hypothesis." When Napoleon reported this exchange to an equally great (but more modest) contemporary mathematician, Joseph-Louis Lagrange, Lagrange responded: "Ah, but it is a fine hypothesis. *It explains so many things*." (14) Napoleon never forgot; in his last days at St. Helena, he commented that Laplace was great mathematician but a poor administrator; in contrast, he said that "Lagrange is the lofty pyramid of the mathematical sciences." [15] Laplace's attitude was, however, fairly typical of scientists up until the 20th century. And, in a muted form, it is still typical of too many scientists today. As we will see, however, Laplace was deeply wrong.

AS ABOVE, SO BELOW?

These things are so bizarre that I cannot bear to contemplate them.

- 19th century mathematician Henri Poincaré. [16]

The first man or woman who stared upwards at the night sky must have wondered about those points of lights. It would have never occurred to them that the earth on which they lived, might not be the center of the universe. In the 2nd century a.d., the Greek astronomer Ptolemy (2nd cent. a.d.) made that speculation explicit, constructing a model of the universe in which a series of clear, perfectly formed, nesting spheres surrounded the earth. The sun, the planets, and the stars rested on those spheres. Since astronomical observations are critical for agriculture, a great deal was already known about the actual positions and movements of the heavenly bodies. But observations had to fit theory, not theory to observations. Since calculations based on Ptolemy's perfect spheres did not fit those observations; more and more complex rationalizations had to be made in order to preserve earth's central position.

Early in the 16th century, Copernicus had the brilliant realization that perhaps the earth was not central and, in fact, the earth was moving around the sun. His view seemed sacrilegious to 16th century churchmen, who were convinced that God had created the world and everything in it in six days. From that time on, the world was static and unchanging, with the known exceptions, such as the Flood, which were recorded in the Bible. For them and for most educated Europeans, Ptolemy's views were merely a scientific explication of what they already knew from the Bible. Knowledge of the world didn't need to come from observation; that knowledge was already contained in the Bible. But eventually Copernicus' view won out. Calculations about the positions and movements of the planets, however, still remained less accurate than desired, in large part it was still assumed that planets moved in circular orbits, rather than the elliptical orbits of Newton's Laws.

Using his new insights, Newton was able to completely solve what mathematicians and astronomers call the "2-body problem." In a universe consisting of only two bodies, say the sun and the earth, Newton could exactly predict the movement of the two bodies. Another century passed, and Laplace's *Mecanique Celeste* attempted to describe the movements of all the planets in the solar system. And, to a great extent, it did. But there were anomalies that didn't always fit into the calculations. Still another century was to pass before the problem was to lead to the beginnings of chaos theory.

In order to celebrate the 60th birthday of King Oscar of Sweden and Norway in 1887, a prize was offered for solving the n-body problem. That is, how to accurately predict the movement of all of the planets. This task proved beyond the power of any mathematician of the time, but the great mathematician Henri Poincaré won the prize in 1899 for his essay on an important piece of the puzzle: the 3-body problem; that is, the complete movement of, for example, earth, sun, and moon. Just as the essay was being set-up as a paper in *Acta Mathematica,* Poincaré realized that it contained a deep and critical error. In correcting this error, Poincaré was able to prove that the complete movement of even three bodies was inherently unpredictable. This discovery shook him so badly that he declared "These things are so bizarre that I cannot bear to contemplate them." Without realizing it, Poincaré had discovered mathematical chaos in the movement of the planets. As with so many seminal discoveries, it was too early for the implications to be fully understood. A new tool was needed: the computer. With it, chaos descended to the earth.

A SHORT HISTORY OF CHAOS THEORY

A violent order is a disorder: and
A great disorder is an order.
These two things are one.

- Wallace Stevens, "Connoisseur of Chaos." (17)

In the early 1960's, Edward Lorenz, a meteorologist at M.I.T., programmed a simple model of the weather. Numbers representing initial weather conditions were input to the program, which then calculated what the weather would be after some interval of time. These results were fed back as initial conditions for the next run, and so on. Using this technique, the computer could predict weather conditions over an extended period of time. (It is important to stress, however, that this was a very simply model, hardly sufficient to deal with all the variables of the weather). Though this was long before computers could present true graphics, people who remember that era of computers might recall that programmers used to have fun by printing pictures using strings of letters instead of lines: Snoopy was a favorite. Though the main output of Lorenz's program were the numbers that described the weather conditions, he used a similar technique to print a continuous paper line graph of those conditions. The line would rise or fall in ways that looked like the movement of the winds or other meteorological phenomena over months or even years.

Since those early computers were very slow, one day he came into the lab, intending to continue the run from the day before. In order to ensure that the results were continuous, he input the initial positions from the middle of the previous day and went off to some other task. He expected that the computer would reproduce identical results from the previous day, then continue on from that point. When he returned to look at the printout, he was shocked to find that the graph looked nothing like the previous day. Initially he thought he must have made a mistake, but when he checked the numeric input, he couldn't find any mistake. Eventually he realized that the only difference between the runs of the two days was that the computer handled calculations using 6 decimals of accuracy, while the printout of numbers, the numbers he had input the next day, only went to 3 decimals. With traditional "static" equations, such a difference would be imperceptible. But since the results of each calculation were fed back as input for the next calculation, over many iterations, those tiny differences could grow until they produced a markedly different result.

Like any good scientist, Lorenz went on to study this puzzling phenomena in a variety of ways involving not only the weather but convection currents in general. Finally, in his words: *"I realized that any physical system that behaved non-periodically would be unpredictable."* (18) Thus was chaos theory borne.

The central issue is that Lorenz was using "dynamic equations" where the results from each run were fed-back into the next run. This was a major advance on how science was done before the computer. The world of mathematics is traditionally a timeless world, in which equations have no direction. Ever since Darwin's discovery of evolution by natural selection, however, scientists realized that they lived in a world in which time could no longer be ignored. Once the arrow of time moved forward, it could not be reversed. But scientists lacked the mathematical tools to deal with the arrow of time. Up until this time, the only mathematical tool for dealing with change over time was calculus. But calculus is also composed of equations which can be calculated either forward or backwards. If you differentiate an equation for distance, you get velocity. Differentiate again and you get acceleration. But you equally start with acceleration, and integrate to get first the equation for velocity, then for distance. With the computer, suddenly relatively simple equations could be used to examine complex situations as they evolved over time, evolved in ways that could no longer be run backwards. As Lorenz found, however, the process of using feedback in a model could produce unexpected results.

Chaos/complexity theory has shown that feedback not only can lead to unexpected change, feedback is also what keeps complex systems (like human beings and heart beats, and stock markets, and most everything else of interest) intact in a changing world. The human body, for example, is constantly feeding information about itself back into itself, so that we can grow yet still retain our identity from childhood to adulthood, even if every single molecule of our body changes over that time. Or take an example familiar to Jungians: the relationship between consciousness and the unconscious is a continuous feedback loop in which each is constantly informing the other. That feedback preserves our identity despite having to face change and adversity. The same feedback can also lead, under certain conditions, to unexpected changes in personality, as, for example, when we have exhausted our conscious resources and find ourselves buffeted by the unconscious.

Though it might be a new discovery for science that feedback underlies both organic closure, and change through the stages of chaos, it was already known in the ancient world through the symbol of the uroboros! And that brings us back to alchemy and Jung's insight in what it shows us about the emergence of consciousness.

SCINTILLAE OF LIGHT

There is a divine spark, the scintilla, indwelling even in dead matter, in utter darkness.

- C. G. Jung. [(19)]

The alchemical image for the darkness, the chaos, that precedes the light of consciousness is the nigredo. It is described as "black, blacker than black," with the additional comment: "and so it is an infinity." (20)

In Jung's "VII Sermones ad Moruos," (Seven Sermons to the Dead), he says similarly:

> Nothing is the same as fullness. In the endless state fullness is the same as emptiness. The Nothing is both empty and full. One may just as well state some other thing about the Nothing, namely that it is white or that it is black or that is exists or that it exists not. That which is endless and eternal has no qualities, because it has all qualities. (21)

So the nigredo is an attempt to express not merely blackness, but something so empty that it is "blacker than black." And at that stage of non-differentiation, nothing is also infinity. It is "both empty and full" because everything is contained within it *in potentia*. It has no qualities yet because only the act of distinction, of discrimination can separate qualities out of this chaos. *This act of making a distinction is the birth of consciousness.* (22)

But something occurs in the chaos that precedes this act of distinction. The alchemists went through a series of steps that first separated then solidified their mixture, over and over through the stages of *solutio* and *coagulatio, sublimatio* and *mortificatio, separatio* and *coniuntio,* with *calcinatio* to heat the mixture at different points. In other words, the solution was fed back onto itself in complex ways, forming the symbol of the uroboros, the snake that swallows its tail. Jung says: "the opus proceeds from the one and leads back to the one, like a dragon biting its own tail." (23) The alchemists already realized that it was this process of feedback through many stages which begin to separate out potential new structure.

Chaos theory has discovered an exact analog of this process, commonly called "the baker transformation." When a baker kneads dough, she flattens it out, folds it upon itself, then flattens and folds again and again. This process has the effect of separating pieces of the dough that originally were close together. Eventually all the points of the dough are separated into an unpredictable pattern. If this process was continued infinitely, the pattern which formed would be what chaos theory calls a *strange attractor;* that is, no point of the dough ever returns to its original position, yet the overall structure is retained.

At some point in this complex feedback process, alchemists reported that they saw scintillae of light in the darkness. Lights would appear and disappear, seemingly at random. Now they weren't really seeing any such thing; these lights were, in Jung's phrase--"visual illusions"--which they had projected onto "the arcane substance;" i.e., they were projecting an inner emergent process out on the experiment they were conducting. The unconscious is ever busy, mixing and re-mixing, trying combinations that form for a time like some primitive consciousness that underlies ego-consciousness. Distinctions come into being, then pass back into the chaos as other distinctions emerge in turn. These scintillae of light that the alchemists saw were the sparks of consciousness that lay below true consciousness. As Jung says: "One would have to conclude from these alchemical visions that the archetypes have about them a certain effulgence or quasi-consciousness, and that numinosity entails luminosity." (24)

"Numinosity entails luminosity." That's quite a pairing, one that has appeared in the religions and mythologies of cultures from the earliest times. In *The Two and the One*, religious historian Mircea Eliade agrees, saying that "light mystically perceived denotes transcendence of this world. . . .It is a certain sign of the revelation of ultimate reality--of reality devoid of all attributes" (25) This was what the alchemists were seeing: ultimate reality, which was "devoid of all attributes" at this point because it had not yet emerged into consciousness. Through their experiments, which were not only chymical experiments, but explorations of their own psyches, they had arrived at a depth of the psyche that transcended ego consciousness. Something was trying to emerge from the collective into their individual psyches, and inevitably, it had a numinous quality. *They saw lights that weren't there because primitive bits of consciousness were forming within their own psyches!*

Now it is important to stress that neither alchemy nor chaos theory *explains* how this new order emerges. Both describe the *process* that leads from an old order to a new. Both describe a process which takes the existing structure, breaks it into pieces, combines the pieces, then repeats this process over and over. In the example we gave at the beginning of the paper of boiling water, it is totally unpredictable which point in the water will become the center around which the final transition to steam forms. The word used over and over in chaos/complexity theory to describe how a new order appears within chaos is *emergence*. Because this is such a descriptive term, it is used and over-used; far too often scientists using it forget that they haven't explained this mysterious process; they have simply named it.

Similarly, alchemy and chaos theory are able to tell us a great deal about the process that must go on before new consciousness can emerge from the unconscious. There is no way to short-circuit this intricate process of feedback. While that process is going on inside, we have the task of holding a tension of opposites within ourselves. Though this is uncomfortable and we would all do almost anything to avoid it, it is necessary. But what the new consciousness that emerges will be is a mystery beyond our understanding. Since this new consciousness might emerge from any unpredictable place within, perhaps the wisest answer is that consciousness, divinity, lives everywhere. Let us close with this beautiful expression of that truth:

God is an intelligible sphere
whose centre is everywhere and
whose circumference is nowhere.

- Alain de Lille, 12th century theologian. [26]

REFERENCES

1. C. G. Jung. *CW8: The Structure and Dynamics of the Psyche* (Princeton: Bollingen Series, Princeton University Press, 1960), par. 412.

2. C. G. Jung, *CW14: Mysterium Coniunctionis, 2nd edition* (Princeton: Princeton University Press, 1970), par. 253

3. Much of this section was reprinted, with minor revisions and adaptions, from Robin Robertson, *Jungian Archetypes*. Nicolas-Hays, Inc., 1995, p. 235-8. Permission was kindly granted by Nicolas-Hays.

4. C. G. Jung, *CW12: Psychology and Alchemy, 2nd edition*, (Princeton: Princeton University Press, 1968), par. 448.

5. John Maxson Stillman, The Story of Alchemy and Early Chemistry, *p. 137.*

6. Marie-Louise von Franz, *Alchemical Active Imagination* (Irving, Texas: Spring Publications, 1979), p. 1.

7. Since Jung's time, much more material has come to light on the wide variety of views lumped under the title of Gnostic. Christianity was just beginning to solidify into the form it would hold for so many centuries, while those with divergent views were united more by their opposition to the ruling ideas than any unity of beliefs. That being said, there is still much to be said for the view

of Gnostics as ancient precursors of modern men and women on a spiritual quest.

8. C. G. Jung, *Memories, Dreams, Reflections, revised edition* (New York: Pantheon Books, 1973), p. 201.

9. Johannes Fabricius, *Alchemy,* Rosenkilde and Bagger, Copenhagen, 1976, p. 7. Other parts of this history were also drawn from Fabricius, pp. 6-7. Perhaps the position of the alchemists was not all that dissimilar from the position of Jungians in our time.

10. Isaac Newton. "The Commentary on the Emerald Tablet." In Stanton J. Linden (ed). *The Alchemy Reader: from Hermes Trismegistus to Isaac Newton* (Cambridge: Cambridge University Press, 2003), p. 247.

11. Alexander Pope, "Intended for Sir Isaac Newton", in Lewis Kroneberger, ed., *Alexander Pope: Selected Works* (New York: The Modern Library, 1951), p. 330.

12. I. Bernard Cohen and Anne Whitman, trans. Isaac Newton, *The Principia: Mathematical Principles of Natural Philosophy* (Berkeley: University of California, Press, 1947), p. 408.

13. E. T. Bell, *Men of Mathematics*. New York, Simon & Schuster, 1937/1965, p. 172.

14. E. T. Bell, *Men of Mathematics,* p. 181.

15. E. T. Bell, *Men of Mathematics,* p. 153.

16. quoted in John Briggs and F. David Peat, *Turbulent Mirror* (New York: Perennial Library, Harper & Row, 1989), p. 29.

17. Wallace Stevens, *The Palm at the End of the Mind* (New York: Vintage Books, 1972), p. 166.

18. James Gleick, *Chaos: Making a New Science* (New York: Viking, 1987), p. 18.

19. C. G. Jung, CW11: Psychology and Religion: West and East, 2nd edition, *(Princeton. Princeton University Press, 1969), par. 152.*

20. Johannes Fabricius, *Alchemy,* p. 98, translating from the Latin of Raymond Lully's *Ultimum Testamentum, Artis aurif., III,* p. 1.

21. C. G. Jung, "VII Sermones ad Moruos," Stephan A. Hoeller, trans., in Stephan A. Hoeller, *The Gnostic Jung and the Seven Sermons to the Dead* (Wheaton, Illinois: A Quest Book, Theosophical Publishing House, 1982), p. 44. See C. G. Jung, *Memories, Dreams, Reflections,* revised edition (New York: Pantheon Books, 1973), appendix V (Septum Sermones ad Mortuos) for a different translation by Richard and Clara Winston.)

22. See Robin Robertson, "The Evolution of Jung's Archetypal Reality." (2000). *Psychological Perspectives #41,* for another way of understanding this act of distinction as presented in logician G. Spencer-Brown's *Laws of Form.*

23. C. G. Jung, CW12: Psychology and Alchemy, *par. 404.*

24. all quotes from C. G. Jung. CW8: The Structure and Dynamics of the Psyche, *par. 388.*

25. Mircea Eliade, *The Two and the One*. New York, Harper & Row, 1965, p. 43-5, excerpted in *Myths, Rites, Symbols, A Mircea Eliade Reader*, Vol. 2. New York & San Francisco, Harper & Row, 1976, p. 333-4.

26. from the *Corpus Hermeticum* of the 3rd Century.

MEMORIES

In late 1899, early 1900, two seminal books were written, each of which in some way created modern depth psychology: Sigmund Freud's *Interpretation of Dreams* and Théodore Flournoy's *From India to the Planet Mars*. Today Freud's book remains a classic while Flournoy's has been unjustly largely forgotten. Things were quite different at the time. Sonu Shamdasani tells us that Flournoy's book, "despite being around twice the size, sold more copies in three months than the former in six years, and swiftly became a best seller." (1)

In *From India to the Planet Mars,* Flournoy analyzed the trance messages that medium Hélne Smith had communicated about life on the Planet Mars, much as Jung later analyzed Wolfgang Pauli's dreams in *Psychology and Alchemy.* (2) Rather than either accepting Smith's messages uncritically, as the spiritualists of the time did, or rejecting them out of hand as fraud, as the scientists of the time (or our time, for that matter) did,

Flournoy instead traced the key elements in Smith's messages back to memory traces unconsciously recovered from her life and reading. He termed the unconscious recovery of hidden memories *cryptomnesia.* "By *cryptomnesia* I understand the fact that certain forgotten memories reappear without being recognized by the subject, who believes to see in them something new." (3)\

Cryptomnesia & Nietzche

Some commentators thought that Flournoy had replaced one unbelievable concept - spirit communication - with another - an essentially limitless memory. In contrast, Jung was quite impressed with Flournoy's ideas and regarded Flournoy, along with Williams James, as his true mentors. In his paper "Cryptomnesia," Jung tells how when reading Nietzche's *Thus Spake Zarathustra,* he came upon a passage where "Nietzche describes how Zarathustra descends into hell through the mouth of a volcano. It seemed to me that I had read this description somewhere before." (4) He couldn't quite place where, but couldn't get it out of his mind. Then he remembered reading a similar story years earlier. When he went back and compared the two versions, there were so many points of agreement that he concluded that Nietzche must have also read the story. One identical point that struck him most was that both mentioned a crew going ashore on an island with a volcano in order to "shoot rabbits." Jung did some research and discovered that, in fact, Nietzche had read this book sometime between the ages of 12 and 15. It wasn't the sort of book one would return to as an adult. And the details were hardly those that Nietzche would have plagiarized. Jung concluded that:

> The normal powers of memory offer no explanation; it is almost inconceivable that Nietzche could have reawakened that old sequence of words by a voluntary act of evocation. The reappearance of old, long-forgotten impressions is, however, explicable in terms of the physiology of the brain. The brain never forgets any impression, no matter how slight; every impression leaves behind it some trace in the memory, no matter how fine. . . . Under special conditions the re-emergence of old memory traces with photographic fidelity is by no means impossible. (5)

The key words here are "special conditions." Rather than being some fantastic ability outside of normal human psychology, cryptomnesia is an extension of normal psychic functions, "under special conditions." In his later book, *Spiritism and Psychology,* Flournoy comments that "it is clear that all our psychic functions - association, reasoning, imagination, etc. - can contribute to this secret elaboration and merit equally the prefix of "crypto." (6) This paper circles around such exceptional memory and the conditions that can bring it about.

Funes, the Memorious

I have more memories in myself alone than all men have had since the world was a world.

- fictional character Ireneo Funes in Borges' "Funes, the Memorious." (7)

In "Funes, the Memorious", Argentinian writer Jorge Luis Borges tells the story of a man, Ireneo Funes, who, after a fall from a horse, found his perception and memory had become essentially limitless.

> On falling from the horse, he lost consciousness; when he recovered it, the present was almost intolerable it was so rich and bright; the same was true of the most ancient and most trivial memories . . . his perception and his memory were infallible. (8)

Where we might walk into the library of a home and see a wall of books, Funes would see every individual book. Not only its author and title (provided they were shown on the edge of the book), but the color and pattern of every book, the wearing at the edges of some books while others were more pristine, the shading of the light that fell on each, their respective positions with respect to other books. And that only mentions the visual. He felt every movement of the air, every tiny change in the pitch of a visitor's voice. The multitude of odors that combine without comment in our own minds were each individually noted by Funes. And everything he perceived, he remembered.

> Locke, in the seventeenth century, postulated (and rejected) an impossible idiom in which each individual object, each stone, each bird and branch had an individual name; Funes had once projected an analogous idiom, but he had renounced it as being too general, too ambiguous. In effect, Funes not only remembered every leaf on every tree of every wood, but even every one of the times he had perceived or imagined it. (9)

Hence not only could Funes perceive every detail of every scene presented to him, but his memory was exact in its self-referential possibilities. That is, he remembered not only everything, not only every context in which it was experienced, but also every context in which that memory came back to mind, thus enriching the original.

As is common in many of his stories, Borges has an unnamed narrator whose tone is so like that of Borges that we can take him to be Borges, thus providing a further air of verisimilitude to the incredible story he tells. Whether his history matches that of the actual Borges is of little concern to Borges, who is also fond of actually naming a character Borges then mixing fictional history with actual autobiography.

At the time he was to meet Funes, the fictional Borges "had begun, not without some ostentation, the methodical study of Latin." Among the Latin volumes he was trying to make his way through was "an odd-numbered volume of the *Historia Naturalis* of Pliny, which exceeded (and still exceeds) my modest talents as a Latinist." (10) Funes heard of Borges possessing these "anomalous books" and sent him a note asking if he could briefly borrow any one of them, together with a Latin dictionary "for I do not know Latin as yet." Full of his own tiny erudition, Borges was, of course, irritated at the effrontery of Funes' assumption that he could make his way through these difficult volumes with only a dictionary, so he sent him the dictionary plus two volumes that exceeded his own capacity, one of which was the Pliny.

When Borges later came to visit Funes, he found him sitting alone in a dark room reciting from memory the Latin books he had read, with Latin original text interspersed with Spanish translation. He didn't yet know that Funes had little need of any company except his prodigious memory. For his visitor, Funes recited stories of fabulous memory which had been told in the single volume of Pliny's *Historia Naturalis* he had been so appropriately loaned. Of course, all those stories faded in comparison with Funes' own memory. As Funes told him, "my memory, sir, is like a garbage disposal". (11)

The Mind of a Mnemonist

Though, of course, no actual memory could quite match that of Funes, A. R. Luria's *The Mind of a Mnemonist: A Little Book about a Vast Memory* (12) records a young Soviet man who came close. The young man worked as a reporter for a local newspaper. When, at the beginning of the day, the editor read the day's assignments to his reporters--"lists of places he wanted covered, information to be obtained in each"--he saw that the young reporter never took notes. When he berated him for this, the reporter calmly repeated the "entire assignment word for word." (13) The editor was so impressed that he sent him to Luria, who was the head of a psychological laboratory, for study.

> When I began my study of S. [as we will call him hereafter in this discussion], it was with much the same degree of curiosity psychologists generally have at the outset of research, hardly with the hope that the experiments would offer anything of particular note. However, the results of the first tests were enough to change my attitude and to leave me, the experimenter, rather than my subject, both embarrassed and perplexed. (14)

Luria gave S. series of different numbers or letters, either reading them out loud or showing them in written form. S. listened closely then repeated exactly what he had heard. With growing excitement, Luria increased the number of items in each series, "giving him as many as thirty, fifty, or even seventy words or numbers." The number of items listed seemed to have no effect on S.'s memory. He could repeat seventy numbers as easily as he had the smaller lists. He could repeat any list forward or backwards with equal alacrity, or tell the word or number before or after any other word or number. He didn't care whether the words were real words or nonsense words. The only requirement was that the words and numbers be pronounced or written clearly, and that there was a pause between each element in the series.

These experiments continued over the following days and weeks, and eventually stretched into years. Luria was to find that S. remembered every one of the tests, every series given on any day in any year. Luria was shocked and "simply had to admit that the capacity of his memory *had no distinct limits* [his emphasis]." [(15)] Both S.'s and Funes' remarkable memories were primarily visual, though as we will see, other senses merged with vision in remarkable ways. Each word, each number brought forth a distinct image, but "for S., there was no distinct line, as there is for others of us, separating vision from hearing, or hearing from a sense of touch or taste. [16] This strange ability--or liability as one views it--is termed *synathesia* from the Greek "syn", meaning "together" and "aisthesis" meaning sensation. Hence sensations mixed together. [17]

When Luria discovered that S.'s astonishing memories were accomplished through a mixture of senses, he began to record the images and other sensations S. associated with various words, numbers, sounds, etc. Tones, for example, brought forth unique visual images for S. He saw a "brown strip against a dark background that had red, tongue-like edges" and had a taste like "sweet and sour borscht" when he heard a 100 decibel, 50cycles/second tone. [18] In case that sounds like the sort of artistic creation that anyone could produce with enough prodding, the compelling fact was that the same sensations would occur whenever that tone occurred. In other words, the tone, the image, the taste were all one for S. The same was true for all his sensations, all his memories.

Nearly all of us have some experience of synesthesia, especially in childhood. Many of us who have ever experienced a "blinding headache" knows how the pain mixes with distinct colored images if we turn our mind inward. When someone talks of "cool" or "hot" colors, we know instinctively at a sensory level what they mean. Marshall McLuhan created a near revolution in thought with his realization that various media were either "cool" or "hot". Children, who are not trapped in the rigidly linear cognitive framework of adults, are quite prone to a mixing of the senses, though nowhere near so markedly as with S. or with others who suffer (?) from synesthesia. In studying patients with synesthesia, neurologist Richard E. Cytowik concluded that "synesthesia is not something that has been added, but has always existed. A multi-sensory awareness is something that has been *lost* from conscious awareness in the majority of people." (19) Cytowik sees synesthetes (as he terms them) as *cognitive fossils,* reminders of the riches that are buried inside our neurological history.

We might think nothing could be more wonderful than to effortlessly remember everything we see, everything we read. Consider the drudgery of the endless childhood drilling in order to memorize vocabulary words, multiplication tables, scientific facts, dates and events in history. For an S. or a Funes, once would be sufficient. So much of our life is dependent on our ability to remember. We might imagine how wonderful to be able to bring forth in conversation perfect quotes from books we had read, exact descriptions of past events that for most of us become muddled.

Another way to view remembering everything, however, is that we forget nothing. And it is often our ability to forget that makes life bearable. "The big question for him [i.e., S.], and the most troublesome, was how he could learn to forget." [20] He found it very difficult to read through a book because each word brought up an image which linked with other images in a nearly infinite regress. Only with difficulty could he pull himself away from the chain of images each word brought up, in order to move through the text. Not only reading but thought itself was prone to the same problem. For every thought was coupled with an image, and every image with other images. Thinking is very difficult if we lose our ability to abstract due to the vividness of the imagery. As Borges says of Funes: "I suspect, nevertheless, that he was not very capable of thought. To think is to forget a difference, to generalize, to abstract. In the overly replete world of Funes there were nothing but details, almost continuous details." [21] Just imagine if all the memories of a lifetime were before you, each as vivid as when they were first experienced. How then do you separate images that never occurred from images that did, if both are equally intense? How even to separate images in your mind from your actual experience of the world. Psychologists refer to children's ability to believe that what they imagine has or will occur as "magical thinking". S. was especially prone to "magical thinking". Though, in his case, it is hard to be certain that he couldn't actually induce the magic.

For example, S. could control his body temperature and heart rate merely by calling up an appropriate image. To accelerate his heart rate, he just imagined himself running after a train; to slow it, he saw himself resting quietly in bed. To raise the temperature of one hand while lowering it in the other, he saw one hand resting on a hot stove, the other holding a piece of ice. Luria, of course, confirmed with tests that this was not merely S.'s imagination.

Though Luria didn't confirm it, S. also claimed to be able to eliminate pain when he was in the dentist's office having his teeth drilled by simply imagine himself standing by watching the drilling. This ability to dissociate from one's primary personality occurs spontaneously in many people under extreme stress. Children with especially traumatic childhood situations may do this to the extent that it creates alternate personalities within, an example of which we will give later.

As S. said of this magical thinking, "to me there's no great difference between the things I imagine and what exists in reality. Often, if I imagine something is going to happen, it does." [(22)] He gave examples of telling a friend that a cashier was going to give him too much change--and later she did. Or he would imagine he could cure himself of illness, or even cure others. He tells a story of a friend's son who experienced stomach pains. S.

remembered the boy had eaten something cooked with lard, so he imagined pieces of the lard in the boy's stomach, then dissolved them in his mind. The boy got better. Though Luria was much more open to considering the existence of unusual abilities than most psychologists of his time (or of our own for that matter), he did not take seriously the possibility that S.'s naive belief that he could control reality with his visualization might actually be true. One wonders.

Memory Act

Are there methods by which normal people can produce a tiny portion of the magical memory feats of S. or Funes? What is needed is a *mnemonic,* which the American Heritage Dictionary defines as "A device, such as a formula or rhyme, used as an aid in remembering." For example, beginning astronomy students memorize the order of the planets from the sun by remembering the phrase: "**M**y **V**ery **E**asy **M**emory **J**ingle **S**eems **U**seful **N**aming **P**lanets" (**M**ercury, **V**enus, **E**arth, **M**ars, **J**upiter, **S**aturn, **U**ranus, **N**eptune, and **P**luto). The classic mnemonic for memorizing how many days are in each month is: "Thirty days hath September/April, June and November/All the rest have thirty-one/except February alone/which has eight and a score/until leap year gives it one day more" (though the latter part of the rhyme has many variants). When I was taking trigonometry, I created a mnemonic of my own to remember the three main trigonometric functions: sine, cosine and tangent. I thought of an Indian Chief named **SOH-CAH-TOA**; i.e., **S**ine = **O**pposite over **H**ypotenuse, **C**osine = **A**djacent over **H**ypotenuse, **T**angent = **O**pposite over **A**djacent.

But let's consider something closer to what S. could do. At one time in my adolescence, when I was doing platform magic, I added a memory act as part of the show. Members of the audience would call out 25 or sometimes 50 objects, which would be listed on a blackboard in the front of the stage. They were allowed to provide quite a lot of detail about an object if they liked. For example, if it was an automobile, they might add that it was a "blue "59 Ford Coupe with a dent in the front right fender." Then, without being able to see the blackboard, I would recite the list from memory, forwards or backwards. When a member of the audience named a number, I would instantly give tell the object at the number. Given an object, I would name the number associated with it.

Though not on the same scale as Funes or S., that sounds pretty miraculous in itself. Alas, I have no particularly remarkable memory; I was using an artificial memory system familiar to magicians. I'll explain that system here, just to show how quickly it can be learned. First, each single digit from 0-9 is associated with one or more consonants. Simple devices are used to make these associations easier to remember. Then two digit numbers are associated with an image by using the two consonants, with appropriate vowels in between, to form easily imaged words. Here's a chart summarizing the associations for the 10 digits from 0-9.

1 = t or d: t has 1 downstroke; t and d sound alike

2 = n: n has 2 downstrokes

3 = m: m has 3 downstrokes

4 = r: four ends in r

5 = l: l is the Roman numeral for fifty, which is like a big five

6 = j or soft g or sh or ch: j looks like a backwards 6; j, sh, ch all sound similar

7 = k or ck or hard g: 7 looks like a key, which starts with k

8 = f or v: 8 looks like a written f, which also sounds like v

9 = b or p: 9 looks like a b or a p turned around or upside down

0 = z or s: 0 is zero, which begins with a z; z and s sound alike

Though many of the mnemonic aids above may seem logically ridiculous, try reading through the list a few times, and see if you don't very quickly remember what letters are associated with what numbers. The next stage is to construct and memorize images for all the 2 digit numbers from 00 to 99. Let's pick one at random, say 25.

2 is associated with n and 5 with l, so we want to make a word which begins with n and ends with l and has only vowels in between (the vowels don't count, only consonants convert to numbers.) For example, "nail" is an easily imagined word. We might imagine a large carpenter's nail, perhaps 6" long. In making these images, the larger and more exaggerated they are, they easier they are to remember. Or we could instead use a finger nail as our image. We'd envision a fist with the index finger sticking out and our attention on a close-up of the finger-nail. Even someone as non-visual as I am can call up such images.

We need to go through all 100 such 2-digit numbers, and construct an image for each which we can easily imagine. It's best to construct our own images rather than just taking a list someone else has created, as the images will stay more firmly in our mind. This might take a while, so start with just 1-10. Use "01", "02", etc. for the single digit numbers. Though as I've said, it's better to construct your own words, here's a list I've made for you:

01: **SuiT** (a suit of clothes on a hanger);

02: **SuN** (a big cartoon sun with rays coming out of it);

03: **SuM** (a sum of numbers on a blackboard);

04: **SiR** (a soldier saluting a General);

05: **SaiL** (a big sail on a sail boat);

06: **SaSH** (a wide ribbon draped across a chest;

07: **SoCK** (a sock with a big hole in the toe);

08: **SaFe** (an old-fashioned safe with a numbered dial);

09: **SoaP** (a bar of soap floating in the bath tub);

10: **ToeS** (a foot with the toes wiggling).

You need to go over the list until when you think of a number you instantly see the image, think of an image and instantly know the number. It takes a little practice, but not nearly as much as learning the multiplication tables, for example. During the learning process, the mnemonic aids serve much as a scaffold does while a building is being constructed. They are helpful in the early stages of learning the list, then are forgotten themselves after the numbers and words become associated directly.

Now only one more mnemonic trick is necessary in order to be able to perform the memory act. When an object is called out by the audience, you imagine a picture which combines an image of the object named with the image associated with that number. For example, if the 5th item was a dog, you might imagine a dog standing up sailing a sail boat. If a book was chosen as the 25th object on the list, you could envision a big carpenter's nail sticking all the way through the middle of a book. At first, you'll need a little time to associate each object, but remember even S. needed a few seconds for each word or number named. You will find that when a number is called later, it instantly brings to mind the combined picture of the image for that number and the object they named. And vice-versa--if they name an object, you automatically know the number. To read back the objects in order, forward or backwards, you merely go through your list forwards or backwards. Again this becomes second-nature.

Finally, how do you remember all the additional details they might add about an object? The answer may surprise you: you don't have to do anything special. Most of the time, those additional details will come to mind without any effort. (23)

Simonides and Artificial Memory

This mnemonic method I have described is peculiar to our own highly abstract time: numbers to letters to words to images. The Greeks and Romans of classical times had a very different method of artificial memory which they developed to a point where those who mastered it came close to rivaling a Funes or an S.

> In 1596 Matteo Ricci taught the Chinese how to build a memory palace. He told them that the size of the palace would depend on how much they wanted to remember: the most ambitious construction would consist of several hundred buildings of all shapes and sizes; "the more there are there the better it will be," said Ricci, though he added that one did not have to build on a grandiose scale right away. One could

> create modest palaces, or one could build less dramatic structures such as a temple compound, a cluster of government offices, a public hostel, or a merchant's meeting lodge. . . In summarizing this memory system, he explained that these palaces, pavilions, divans were mental structures to be kept in one's head, not solid objects to be literally constructed out of "real" materials. (24)

The above quotation describes the method used by the Greeks and Romans which continued to be used in the Western world through the Renaissance. By custom it was assumed to have been discovered by the poet Simonides of Ceos in the 5th-6th century B.C. The story goes that a nobleman named Scopas was giving a banquet. He commissioned Simonides to compose and chant a lyric poem in his honor, which also praised the legendary twins Castor and Pollux. When Simonides delivered the poem, Scopas evidently felt the twins had received more praise than he had intended, as he gave the poet only half his fee, telling him to get the rest from the gods.

A few minutes later Simonides was called out of the banquet to talk to two men (?) who wanted to see him. Outside he found no one waiting to talk to him. While he was outside, however, the roof collapsed, killing everyone inside. The destruction was so devastating that the relatives who came couldn't even identify the bodies.

But Simonides was able to remember where everyone had been sitting, so their identities could be determined from the location of their bodies. As scholar Frances Yates notes, "Castor and Pollux had handsomely paid for their share in the panegyric by drawing Simonides away from the banquet just before the crash". [25] Realizing how significant the mind's memory of place was, Simonides determined to develop a memory system drawing on that seemingly native ability. You might imagine a room which you enter through a door, then move around in a fixed pattern. As you walk around the room in your mind (clockwise we'll say), you imagine visual images of the words to be memorized in the various locations you visit. In order to later remember the words in order, you had only to move through the room in your mind, noting the objects that have been placed there.

In more complete version of the system, a simple mental room could grow to a house, to a palace, to a town if necessary, all depending on the number of words to be memorized. Classical orators memorized entire speeches this way. Most often, they assigned key words for parts of their speech, allowing themselves to extemporize around those key words, but some memorized every word of a lengthy oration using this technique. And if that still seems a little tame, consider the 16th century preacher Francesco Panigarola, who "was described by acquaintances in Florence as being able to roam across a hundred thousand memory images, each in its own fixed space." (26) Though this method of place was artificially developed, it is clearly based on an apparently inherent ability of the mind to remember places we visit. Luria's wondrous S. used this technique in remembering his lists.

> When S. read through a long series of words each word would elicit a graphic image. And since the series was fairly long, he had to find some way of distributing these images of his in a mental row or sequence. Most often (and this habit persisted throughout his life), he would "distribute" them along some roadway or street he had visualized in his mind. (27)

When he later became a stage mnemonist, and daily had to remember thousands of words and numbers to satisfy his audience, he tidied up this method a bit. "The device he developed was a shorthand system for his images." Before, when he simply relied on his incredible visual imagery, the images he remembered were incredibly rich and varied, filled with every detail imaginable. Now he made the images cruder. "I just try to single out the details I'll need to remember a word." (28) It's easy to see here how the natural methods of memory begin to blend with the artificial methods.

Memories as Creative Acts

The variety of examples of memory we've presented in this article seem to imply that we remember everything, but may or may not be able to recover those memories. Some come to the surface without our knowledge through the process of cryptomnesia. Some special people like Borges' Funes or Luria's S. seem to be able to have access to the totality of their memories. We've seen that mnemonic methods allow normal people like you and me to remember astonishing amounts of information. And those mnemonic methods seem to be a part of the explanation of how people like S. do store and recall much of their memories. Neuro-science has increasingly turned its focus on memory in recent times, but we still don't understand this process very thoroughly. It's possible that saying that we seemingly remember everything is a slight overstatement of the situation, but it's undoubtedly closer to the real situation than any of the descriptions of memory we learned in school.

For example, tests have been conducted to measure the difference between what we recall when we try to, and what we simply recognize. "In one experiment subjects were presented with a list of one hundred words five times. When asked to recall the list, they scored about 30 percent. When, on the other hand, the subjects were asked to recognized the one hundred words mixed with one hundred unrelated words they scored 96 percent correct. This still leaves open the possibility that under more suitable experimental conditions they would have recognized even more, perhaps even 100 percent. . . . It was also seen that visual memory is considerably superior to verbal memory. On tests of ten thousand pictures, subjects recognized 99.6 percent of them correctly." As one researcher commented: "The recognition of pictures is *essentially perfect.*" (29) In recent days, cognitive psychologists like to use the computer as the metaphor for how the mind works. In this vastly over-simplified analogy, the brain is analogous to the hardware (i.e., the computer) and memories are like software (i.e., programs). But memory doesn't seem to work that way. Instead of pulling out a permanently static memory, like a computer does a program, the mind seems to dynamically recreate the memory out of the total memory structures recorded in the brain. This recreation of the memory is itself also stored in the brain and becomes linked with the original memory through the act of recall. As we recall an event multiple times, this process of progressively recreating the memory, means that we are recalling not only the original event, but all the times we have remembered it before. Over time, memories can become quite colored by those instances of remembering them, much like the way rumors can change drastically as they pass from one person to another.

At this moment I'm typing words on a word-processor. I'm conscious of the words on the monitor in front of me. Usually when I'm writing, that is virtually all that I'm conscious of. I don't hear the drone of the fan in my computer (which is quite loud). I don't hear the softer purr of the air conditioner in the background. I'm not aware of the way my body feels in the chair I sit in (until I sit so long that I realize I ache all over). I don't see the books to the right and left of the monitor, or the wall of books behind it. In short, I'm not conscious of most of the sensations with which I'm constantly bombarded.

Yet all of the other sensations - sights, sounds, smells, temperature changes on my skin, etc. - are noticed by my body. And, seemingly, virtually all of them are somehow recorded. Jungian analyst and hypnotherapist Ernest Lawrence Rossi has summarized a wide variety of research that argues persuasively that our memories are "state dependent." [30] Much like Borges' Funes, we don't remember isolated little bits of information, we remember the entire environment in which an event took place. Because of this fact, it's often quite difficult to remember an event in a totally different physical environment. However, if we return our body and mind to a state similar to the state they were in when an event first took place, we can usually re-experience that event as if it were taking place right now. A classic example is the rich man in the Charlie Chaplin movie *City Lights*. Time after time, whenever he's drunk, he loves the tramp. When he's sober, he doesn't even recognize him. Chaplin uses this to brilliant comic effect, but the switch between one state and another is not all that different from how state-dependent memory actually works. (31) The fact that all memory thus seems to be creative fits closely with Jung's example of how Nietzche unconsciously incorporated details of a consciously long-forgotten book of childhood into perhaps his most important book.

If memories are not merely retrieved over and over from some storage bin, but actively created, it also explains how false memories arrive. Hypnotherapists have to be especially careful not to induce false memories, through suggestion which the patient's mind combines with actual memory to produce a false memory that seems absolutely real. We've seen the worst results of this in the proliferation of false memories of childhood sexual abuse. This is one of those areas, much like the nature/nature arguments, where the pendulum continues to swing too widely to one side or the other of the argument. In Freud's 1996 paper, "The Etiology of Hysteria," he told how he had discovered memories of infantile sexual abuse in eighteen patients. Later, largely because he simply couldn't believe that so many fathers could have abused their children, he changed his mind and decided that these were not actual memories but instead caused by repressed sexual fantasies. This led to the conclusion that all such memories were merely repressed fantasies.

In our own time, we have come to realize that childhood sexual abuse is not uncommon and the memories Freud dismissed as fantasy were all too often far too real. Unfortunately, with that realization, some therapists have gone too far in the other extreme and, with no evil intention in mind, have created false memories of childhood sexual abuse. A similar pattern has happened with recovered memories of satanic rituals and alien abductions. Because of these excesses, some critics have argued that all "recovered memories" are fabrications caused by the therapist. Of course, they are also going too far. This whole area is complex and deserves deep thought.

I'd like to close with an example from my experience with a patient, who I'll call Sally, in which all her memories were "recovered memories," and hopefully none were created by me. Sally had a terrible childhood with a mother who presented a kind, loving face to the world, but behind closed doors abused her two children in virtually every way possible. Sally's younger brother finally broke under the pressure and committed suicide. When that happened, a new personality came into existence in Sally, one she called "the Android." The Android served as an intermediate personality between Sally and life, much like the screeners on radio talk shows who prevent the more disturbing callers from reaching the host. Like Data on "Star Trek: Next Generation" many years later (at least until Data got his emotion chip), the Android felt no emotion at all and only fed a neutered version of reality on to Sally. This protected Sally from her mother's worst excesses so that Sally survived until adulthood. However, you can't live without full emotional involvement for a lifetime without suffering the consequences.

When I first saw Sally, she had attempted suicide the previous week by swimming out to sea. When she was far enough out, she let herself go under and drown--and in fact she felt convinced that she had drowned. The following morning, however, she woke up alive on a beach some miles away, where the sea had gently deposited her. The Android had vanished, never to return. Sally felt as if she had been almost literally reborn. Like any newborn, everything was new and strange to her; she had no conscious memories when she first came out of the water. This was so pronounced that she would often find herself wondering what even normal objects were. For example, while brushing her hair that week, she stopped and stared at the hair brush, wondering what it was.

Gradually, her memories did come back, bit by bit, and somehow this reborn Sally was able to deal with her terrible past. I think that a healing had gone on during that night of death at sea and rebirth on the shore, because the entire process was like a long-term therapy compressed into little more than six months. All the ups-and-downs, refusals to accept, the break-throughs, the regressions, that normally comes so slowly during therapy happened in "quick-time," so to speak. Sally went back into the world fully healed, emotions intact, having even worked through her anger and hatred at her mother. Key here is that for her, all memories were "recovered." Now it's possible that the reborn Sally re-created and in the process modified the memories such that they could be accepted emotionally. But I must admit that I don't believe it. I think she found a way, a drastic way, to heal herself.

Thus we end our discourse on memory much as we started, with mystery and awe. And we haven't even touched on archetypal memory. I'll give the final words to a supreme materialist and an avant garde poet.

Memory is the primary and fundamental power, without which there could be no other intellectual operation.

- Samuel Johnson.

Memories are hunting horns, whose noise dies away in the wind.

- Guillaume Appolinaire.

REFERENCES

1. Sonu Shamdasani, *Jung and the Making of Modern Psychology,* Cambridge: Cambridge University Press, 2003, p. 128.

2. C. G. Jung, *Collected Works, Vol. 12: Psychology and Alchemy, 2nd ed.,* Princeton: Princeton University Press, Bollingen Series XX, 1968.

3. *Théodore Flournoy,* From India to the Planet Mars: A Case of Multiple Personality with Imaginary Languages, *Princeton, Princeton University Press, 1899/1994, p. 8.*

4. C. G. Jung, C. G. Jung, "Cryptomnesia," *Collected Works, Vol. I:Psychiatric Studies, 2nd ed.,* Princeton: Princeton University Press, Bollingen Series XX, 1970, par. 180.

5. C. G. Jung, "Cryptomnesia," par. 183.

6. Théodore Flournoy, *Spiritism and Psychology,* New York and London: Harper & Bros. Publishers, 1911, p. 114.

7. Jorge Luis Borges, "Funes, the Memorious", in *Ficciones* (English edition, New York: Grove Press, 1962), p. 112.

8. Borges, "Funes, the Memorious", in *Ficciones,* p. 112.

9. Borges, "Funes, the Memorious", pp. 113-114.

10. Borges, "Funes, the Memorious", p. 109.

11. Borges, "Funes, the Memorious", p. 112.

12. A. R. Luria, *The Mind of a Mnemonist: A Little Book about a Vast Memory* (English translation, Cambridge, Massachusetts and London, England: Harvard University Press, 1968).

13. Luria, The Mind of a Mnemonist, *p. 8.*

14. Luria, The Mind of a Mnemonist, *p. 9.*

15. Luria, The Mind of a Mnemonist, *p. 11.*

16. Luria, The Mind of a Mnemonist, *p. 27.*

17. Luria, The Man Who Tasted Shapes, *p. 5.*

18. Luria, The Mind of a Mnemonist, *p. 23.*

19. Cytowic, The Man Who Tasted Shapes, *p. 167.*

20. Luria, The Mind of a Mnemonist, *p. 67.*

21. Borges, "Funes, the Memorious", p. 115.

22. Luria, The Mind of a Mnemonist, *p. 146.*

23. See Al Baker, *Magical Ways and Means, 2nd edition* (Minneapolis: Carl Waring Jones, Publisher of Magic, 1946), pp. 96-98. Baker uses a different association between the letters and numbers than I have presented here.

24. Jonathan Spence, *The Memory Palace of Matteo Ricci* (New York: Penguin, 1984), p. 1.

25. Frances Yates, *The Art of Memory* (Chicago: University of Chicago Press, 1966), p. 2.

26. Yates, The Memory Palace of Matteo Ricci, *p. 9.*

27. Luria, The Mind of a Mnemonist, *pp. 31-2.*

28. both quotes from Luria, *The Mind of a Mnemonist*, p. 42.

29. Peter Russell, *The Brain Book,* New York: Hawthorn Books, 1979, pp. 163-4.

30. see Ernest Lawrence Rossi, *The Psychobiology of Mind-Body Healing,* New York: W. W. Norton & Company, 1986, pp. 36-56, for a summary of the past research in this area.

31. Marilyn Ferguson, *The Brain Revolution,* New York: Taplinger Publishing Company, 1973: p. 72.

VISIONS OF THE MILLENNIUM

HOPI/MAYAN PROPHESIES OF THE "END TIMES"

Beginning with their Genesis, and carrying through their Old Testament of previous worlds, and their New Testament of the present to the Revelation of their esoteric ceremonialism, the tenets of these books are as sacred to the Hopis as the Judaic-Christian Bible is to other people.

- *Frank Waters,* Book of the Hopi. (1)

The world has grown so complex, so vague and ambiguous, that it sometimes seems beyond any individual's ability to understand, much less to control. The brave dreams of our Victorian ancestors-so convinced that they were on the verge of solving all the mysteries, conquering all the demons that had held us captive for so long-have grown stale and crumbled into dust. Once the theme of "progress" seemed an anthem that would lead us forthrightly (and self-righteously) into a glorious future of unending achievement; now progress has stalled and advance has yielded to retreat. The mood has passed from optimism to pessimism, then to despair and, most recently, to either a greedy hedonistic apathy or a split in values so extreme that there seems no possibility of reconciliation.

Yet on the horizon looms a sight so glorious and strange that we don't even have mental categories to encompass the vision. In one of Colin Wilson's books, he tells the story (perhaps apocryphal) of Captain James Cook's arrival in the South Seas. When Cook's great three-masted ships appeared on the horizon, the islanders could not see the ships. They literally could not see the ships and were startled when the white men appeared on their shores. Without some concept of such a ship, they could not find a mental compartment adequate for the strange sight before them, and so they saw nothing at all. Like the islanders, today we stare at visions that fill the entire field of sight and somehow manage to blank them out and see nothing at all.

All over the world, people are trying to contain these strange visions in some way. Change is never welcome, and when nothing but disaster is expected, all change appears to portend disaster. If the world isn't going to die of starvation, it will blow itself up. If the economic structure of the world isn't going to collapse, leaving the rich richer and the poor dead, then the reverse will happen: the undeveloped nations will become so powerful that the current world-powers will become second-rate has-beens. If the dictators don't get us, the terrorists will. We've heard so many terrible scenarios that we just sit numbly, expecting the worst. Yet all of these are just attempts to explain the previous unexplainable. When the familiar disappears, how else to try and explain the new?

All over the world, prophets are arising, reminding us of the old prophesies of world's end, or crying new prophesies to fit our times. All seem so close to our circumstances that we shiver and intellectualize them out of our sight, trying in our tired, frightened way to exorcize the demons that threaten to swallow us.

HOPI HISTORY

The Hopis first released information about their history, myths, legends, and religious ceremonies-all of which form a single entity for the Hopis-to Frank Waters, who published them in his *Book of the Hopi* in 1963. However, the Hopis revealed only part of their mysteries at that time. More recently, they have chosen to release additional information through a variety of spokesmen, including members of other tribes, "breeds", even whites. However, to understand the Hopi prophesies, we have to understand something of the Hopis.

The Hopis are an isolated, introverted, mysterious people, living alone on the plateaus of Arizona, surrounded by their numerous out-going neighbors: the Navajos. Most anthropologists think that the Hopis were a Mongolian people who crossed the then-existent land bridge over the Bering Strait twelve hundred years ago, and then migrated southward. Tree-ring analysis shows that their three main settlements at Oraibi in Arizona were first settled over seven hundred years ago. The Hopis have lived there in their splendid isolation ever since.

The Hopis' own histories tell a very different story. According to Waters, they assert that they made a great ocean crossing, passing over a series of "stones" (i.e., islands), thousands of years ago. They didn't come from the North and migrate southward; they entered in Middle America and migrated northward. The medicine chief I studied with said that, in histories not revealed to Waters, the Hopis tell of the time before this migration, when an earlier migration was made: *from the stars*. These histories say that their ancestors came from the Dog Star Sirius one hundred and eighty thousand years ago. Interestingly, the Dogon, an African tribe with no known connection with the Hopis, also believe that their ancestors came from Sirius. The Dogon are also aware that Sirius has a "twin star" not visible to the naked eye, a fact not known to modern science until 1862.

In favor of the anthropologists' theory is the fact that every Hopi child is born with the Mongolian spot at the base of their spine, which seems irrefutable evidence that the Hopi, like their probable cousins, the Mayans, are Mongolian in origin. Other evidence, however, favors the Hopis' version of history and argues that their Mongolian ancestors came to the Americas long before the land bridge across the Bering Strait came into existence . For example, fossil remains have placed men on the North American continent over twenty thousand years ago. In addition, analysis of blood groupings show that Native Americans have the purest "Type-O" blood groups in existence. This would mean that Native Americans were isolated from their ancestors much longer ago than anthropologists would have us believe. Frank Waters says:

> There is a great body of literature, ever growing from antiquity to the present, asserting that sea crossings were made from Asia to America centuries before the Vikings and Columbus arrived from across the Atlantic. The earliest of these is the most ancient Chinese classic, Shan Hai King, compiled about 2250 B.C. It describes a voyage across the 'Great Eastern Sea' and a two-thousand-mile journey down the length of the land beyond. Long regarded as a book of myth, it is now asserted to be an accurate geographic description of various landmarks in America including the "Great Luminous Canyon" now known as Grand Canyon.

WORLDS OF CONSCIOUSNESS

According to Waters, the Hopis' histories/mythologies talk of four successive worlds, each destroyed by a great catastrophe, after each of which men emerged into a new world. To the Hopis, the destruction of these "worlds" is - at one and the same time - both literal and symbolic. The "worlds" represent both stages of consciousness and epochs of human history. At each stage, there is both a collective state of consciousness within the world and a corresponding personal state of consciousness within each person. The latter correspond to particular psycho-physical locations in the human body, which are identical in location and general function to the Hindu chakras. We are now living at the end of the fourth world, which corresponds to the most material, the least spiritual, of the four worlds. It is the nadir; when it ends, a higher series of worlds begins.

According to Waters, after their "emergence" into the fourth world at the " Tuwanasavi" [i.e., Center of the Universe] - which is located at the current site of Hopi settlements in Arizona - the Hopis split into four groups or clans, each of which went off to either the north, east, south, or west. Their task was to journey until they reached the sea, then return to their starting point. Having completed one "round", they would start in a new direction and again make a full round-trip. They were to proceed thus either clock-wise or counter-clockwise until they completed all four "rounds". Their journeys would have formed a great cross or swastika about the Tuwanasavi, where they could come together in a permanent settlement, free of clan arguments or differences.

They left pictorial records-"glyphs"-of their migrations on rocks throughout the Americas. Mayan glyphs can be readily read by Hopis, which buttresses the Hopis' claim that both had common ancestors. These pictorial records describe clearly how many of their four journeys each group had taken, and the order in which they were taken. Only the record at Oraibi, the home of the Hopi, shows all four migrations completed.

> The symbol found at Chichen Itza [author's note: the capital of the Mayan empire; a city which-like Babylon-became the capital of successive empires, each time to be abandoned and later rediscovered] indicates that the people covered only one round before returning to the same area and attests to the Hopi belief that the Mayans were simply aberrant Hopi clans who did not complete their migrations. (2)

> The Emergence and the migrations are so beautiful in concept, so profoundly symbolic, one is tempted to accept them wholly as a great allegory of man's evolutionary journey on the Road of Life. . . . It is difficult to reconcile a people having such an

enlightened concept of spiritual life with an actual primitive people wandering over a vast and undiscovered continent in prehistoric times. Yet such were the Hopis. Archeological remains and ancient records attest this. (3)

HOPI RELIGION

Traditional Hopis live in isolation in Oraibi, shrinking in numbers, preserving their heritage, their magical teachings. They believe that by practicing their beliefs, they keep the world in balance. They have no priesthood because every male Hopi serves as priest at one or another of their ceremonies during the year "after which he returns to work in his fields, wearing no vestige of priestly garb and carrying no aura of sanctity."

The Hopis live a life so thoroughly entwined with religion that modern Westerners may have a difficult time grasping it. The Hopis view religion on both the abstract level and the literal level simultaneously, rather than falling into literalistic interpretation or dismissing religion with abstract interpretation. This combination seems - to Western eyes - either primitive or profound depending on our willingness to accept their very different view of reality. Linguist Benjamin Whorf studied the Hopi language and found that it exhibited the same complexity. He comments that "the Hopi thought world has no imaginary space . . . it may not locate thought dealing with real space anywhere but in real space, nor insulate space from the effects of thought."

That duel level of acceptance is most clearly expressed in their prophesies. The Hopis have studied these prophesies, which are spread over the walls of special underground chambers called *kivas* (literally "world below"), sacred places where the Hopis hold their religious rituals. During the Hopis' ancient migrations, "they had no homes save small pits they dug in the earth and roofed over with brush and mud." Like virtually everything else in the Hopi culture, these kivas evolved into both a practical solution to their need for a gathering place and a symbolic representation of their articles of faith.

> Cylindrical or rectangular, it was sunk deep, like a womb, into the body of Mother Earth, from which man is born with all that nourishes him. A small hole in the floor symbolically led down into the previous underworld, and the ladder-opening through the roof symbolically led out to the world above. [(4)]

> The kiva is thus the focal point of Hopi life. It abstractly symbolizes the tenets of the ancient ceremonies performed in it; it functions on the secular level; and it is the underground heart of all that is truly, distinctively Hopi. [(5)]

Others may visit many of the sacred sites of the Hopi - visitors frequently tour other more pedestrian kivas, but not these particular sacred caves, where the ancient teachings are recorded. Like all such ancient knowledge, the prophesies are expressed in symbols and, hence, are open to interpretation, but the Hopi have had nothing but time to carefully study and interpret these writings. They were willing to withdraw into seclusion originally because the teachings told them that this would be necessary, that the white man would rule over the Indian for this long time.

TIME OF PURIFICATION

In 1987, Michael Toms interviewed John Kimmey, a white man whom the Hopi elders picked to spread their message, on New Dimensions radio. Almost twenty years earlier, fresh out of the armed forces, Kinney visited what he later found to be a "sacred place" in Northern California. While there, he experienced the earth "speaking" to him. He returned to the spot many times. During one visit, he "heard" two words: "Taos" and "Oraibi." (6) He vaguely knew Taos was a town in New Mexico, but had never heard of Oraibi: the village in Arizona where the Hopi Indians have lived continuously (almost entirely in peace) since before 1150 a.d.

Kimmey went to Oraibi and told his story to an elder (a "grandfather" in Native American terms). Shortly afterwards, in Taos he found the teacher he was intended to find: "Little Joe" Gomez, with whom he lived and studied for eight years. Upon Little Joe's death, Kimmey acquired a Hopi "grandfather." Since then, Kimmey has been both a student of the Hopi elders and a teacher of the Hopi children. He is an adopted Hopi and has been delegated by the Hopi to spread the Hopi prophesies.

In Kimmey's description of the Hopi prophesies, the time of "purification" (that is, the critical time of passage from one world to the next) would be announced by

> . . . a "gourd of ashes" which is spilled upon the earth. This ash will be poison. Everything will burn for a great distance around that area and nothing will grow there for a long time. The ashes will get into the water and air. People who drink the water will soon die. Women who are exposed to it will not be able to give normal birth. (7)

In 1946, the first atomic test explosion took place in Almagordo, New Mexico. When the Hopis heard about the bomb, they knew this was the "gourd of ashes" which would announce the time of purification. In 1947 they convened a meeting of the elders of all the clans in Hopiland, in order to synthesize all their varied knowledge of Hopi teachings and prophesies into a single version they could present to the world, as their prophesies had told them they must. Though Frank

Waters discusses none of this, it undoubtedly figured in the Hopis decision to share some of their knowledge with him.

Kimmey says that the Hopis predict three great symbolic " shakings" of the earth. The first is symbolized by the Swastika, the ancient masculine symbol. The swastika is an ancient symbol that first appeared as early as the Bronze Age. Until adopted by the Nazi party in World War II, it was an honored symbol with deep religious significance for virtually all early traditions except the Egyptians. The Swastika was also the pattern described by the migratory routes which the Hopis and Mayans took when they arrived in the Americas. The Hopi "grandfathers" interpreted World Wars I and II as the predicted "masculine" upheaval; the Nazi Swastika was for them a proof of this interpretation. The Hopis saw these terrible wars as evidence of the trouble caused when the masculine principle, with its inherent need for aggression and expansion, is cut-off from the gentle receptivity and containment of the feminine principle.

The second "shaking" of consciousness was symbolized by the sun, which the Hopis regard as the symbol of the feminine because they view the sun as the mother of the earth. After much reflection, the Hopi "grandfathers" have concluded that the Western world's "continuing dialog with the Eastern hemisphere" (the land of the "rising sun") marks this second, feminine upheaval. Obviously, as evidenced by our wars in Korea and Vietnam, the West's response to the East has largely been negative. On the other hand, Japan's integration of Western ways into their Eastern culture marks a positive aspect of the dialog, as does the spread of Eastern fields of study such as Zen, Vedanta, Aikido, etc. in the West.

The third great "shaking" of the world is symbolized by the " red hat and red cloak people." They can either bring us wisdom which we accept or they can destroy us. Kimmey says that "the Hopi people are very cautious about interpreting [this symbol] because we are in the midst of it." A "purification" must inevitably occur, which will cleanse the remains of the "fifth world" to prepare for the "sixth world." [The "fifth world" occupies only a brief period following the longer four worlds discussed by Waters]. (8) The outcome of the third shaking is, however, ambiguously presented: either of two resolutions can occur. One possibility is a successful union of the male and female principles, which the Hopis view as following the inborn, instinctual plans set in each of us at birth by "the Great Spirit." The other possibility is, of course, that we can use the "gourd of ashes" to wipe out all life. If we take that path, the Hopis say that the world will be decimated in a single day, and "the ants" will be left to rule the world.

Happily, one of the signs which presaged a more positive resolution has already occurred. The Hopis predicted that a representative of the "red hat and red cloak people" would send a representative to share their wisdom with the Hopis. The Tibetan lamas - who wear red hats and cloaks - also have prophesies of the time of "purification." These said that "in the time when the iron bird flies and the iron horse rides on rails," they would be exiled from their land and scattered over the earth. At that time, they must go to the place of the "red-faced people" to "plant the seed of the Dharma." Acting upon these prophesies, the exiled Dali Lama consulted his oracles to find where among the "red men" the wisdom should be taken; the oracles said: "go to the Hopis."

A representative of the Tibetans - Go Man Kin Rimpoche - was sent to Hopiland. The Hopi grandfathers asked if, in his trips among Zen centers, etc. in the Unites States, he had seen any who had successfully merged the masculine and the feminine. Sadly, he said "no;" many were striving to join the two sides, but he concluded that cultural difference prevented the Americans from being able to successfully use the Eastern teachings. Because of this, the Dali Lama considered the Native Americans as offering the best chance of saving the world.

I'm reminded of the story Wordsworth tells of crossing the alps in his epic poem: "The Prelude." Wordsworth and a friend went on a walking tour of the alps. Both looked forward with anticipation to the point when they would reach the peak of the alps. But their journey took them alternately up and then down so many times that they wondered when they would ever reach the top. They stopped a peasant and asked him how far it was to the top. He kept pointing back in the direction they had come from. Though there was some difficulty with language, they were finally made to understand "that we had crossed the Alps." The Hopis see the point of passage from the "fifth world" to the "sixth world" in similar terms. Perhaps in hope of this better outcome, we might add these further words from "The Prelude."

Our destiny, our being's heart and home,
Is with infinitude, and only there;
With hope it is, hope that can never die,
Effort, and expectation, and desire,
And something evermore about to be. (9)

2012 MAYAN PROPHESIES

Paradoxically, despite achieving great sophistication in architecture, sculpture, art, road building, writing, numerical calculation, calendar systems and predictive astronomy, the Mayans never invented the wheel, never discovered metal or glass, had no clocks which could measure time intervals of less than a day, and never made use of beasts of burden. Stone Age practices went hand in hand with extraordinary arithmetical sophistication.

- John D. Barrow. (10)

In recent years, there has been a spate, I might even say a surfeit, of books and articles predicting enormous changes, for good or evil, in the year 2012. The largest portion of these are based on interpretations of Mayan prophesies. To very briefly summarize the core of all these interpretations, the Mayans had a complex calendar system referred to as the *Long Count*, based on an equally complex numbering system. It appears that the mathematically sophisticated concept of *zero* was independently discovered in the New World by the Mayans as well as in India at approximately the beginning of the Christian era, though the discovery may well have first occurred as many as several centuries earlier. It enters into the predictions based on the long count as we'll see. (11)

Frank Waters, whose views on the Hopis we have already discussed at some length, wrote of the Mayans that "No other people on earth have been so obsessed with time. Our imaginations balk at the astronomical figures of their mathematical calculations." (12) Where we consider days, weeks, months, years, centuries and perhaps millennia, the Mayans thought of time in much larger terms. They used *kin* (days), a 20 day *uninal* (a sort of semi-month), 18 giving a 360 day *tun* (year), a *katun* (20 years), a *baktun* (20 katun), and a world age cycle of 13 baktun. They also had *pictuns* (20 baktuns), *calabtuns* (20 pictuns), *kinchiltuns* (20 calabtuns), *alautuns* ((20 kinchiltuns), on and on up to a *hablatun*, which would translate into 460.8 billion days; i.e., nearly 1.3 billion years. [(13)]

Note that the exception to the multiplication by twenty of 18 uninals was to make it align with the 360 day year. This is in part a problem caused by their use of a twenty digit number system rather than our own ten digit system. They were quite aware of the actual period of the solar year to a degree of sophistication unique at that point in time and had a 365 day year for solar purposes.

If we represent Mayan dates, substituting our normal number symbols with periods for place values instead of the symbols and place values used by the Mayans, any Mayan date can then be calculated on our own calendar. Using that modification of the Mayan notation, the beginning of the Long Count would be 0.0.0.0.0 (hence all zeros, the beginning of the most recent World Age for the Mayans); modern scholars have calculated that date to be August 11, 3114 B.C. The end of the current world age would be 13.0.0.0.0, which equals December 21, 2012. That's the key date that has so many so excited. It's important to realize that the Mayans didn't think the world begin on 0.0.0.0.0 or ended on 13.0.0.0.0. On various shrines, they had dates extending both before the beginning date and after the end of the long count. [(14)] For example, archaeologist Guillermo Bernal of Mexico's

National Autonomous University points out that at other Mayan sites, there are dates far beyond 2012, including one that roughly translates to the year 4772. (15)

It's regarding this date for the end of the current world age that commentators ("twentytwelveologists" in John Major Jenkins' wonderful coinage) take every possible position from arguing that this means absolutely nothing to, at the other extreme, crying out like Chicken Little that on that day we're all doomed. A 2009 sci-fi movie, "2012," took the "we're all doomed" point-of-view to its extreme, with special effects showing the entire earth destroyed by cataclysmic earthquakes, floods, and fires. Despite poor critical reviews, it was a worldwide success. It's no wonder that books taking the same point-of-view have been more successful than those drawing more on facts. The current Mayans themselves are alternately bewildered and/or bored by this Western version of apocalypse being projected onto their calendar. (16)

Beyond the arithmetic of the Long Count itself, things can get very complicated, with calculations showing how this exact point in time also corresponds to a global convergence between the December solstice sun and the Galactic center of the Milky way. This isn't as mystical as it sounds, as Jenkins and others point out: the Mayan New Year was defined at the Winter Solstice, and their calendar was developed on the basis that it would reach round numbers on those days. This particular convergence though is indeed rare: an event that occurs only once every 25,800 years; i.e., after five Long Counts, five world ages. And that brings us to Frank Waters and a "coming sixth world of consciousness."

In *Mexico Mystique: the Coming Sixth World of Consciousness*, Frank Waters drew on these prophesies, largely as recorded in the Mayan's sacred book, the *Popol Vuh*. According to Jenkins:

> [Waters's] observations in his book *Mexico Mystique* are those of a mature, elder philosopher, presented in sure-handed tones. . . .It was patently clear to him that the Baktun cycle was part of a World Age Doctrine . . . Waters's book was the first one dedicated to the end-date question, and he can be considered the man who launched the 2012 phenomenon. [17]

His book has been largely overlooked by later twentytwelveologists because Waters made use of a calculation for the starting and ending date of the world age that has later been superceded by further scholarship. He had the end date in 2011. But his book is unmatched for the richness of understanding of the culture not only of the Mayans but of both their ancestors and successors: Olmecs, Zapotecs, Mixtecs (and perhaps Hopis).

We earlier discussed the Hopi belief that the Mayans were aberrant Hopis who hadn't fully completed the four full rounds of migrations that formed the sacred Swastika. In studying the Mayan prophesies, Waters was able to draw on his knowledge of Hopi culture and mythology to counter-balance his scholarly research into Mayan history and tradition. There were many points of agreement. We don't need to decide whether the Hopis were right about the Mayan origin, or whether the Hopis were themselves descendants of Mayans. His interpretation of the Mayan prophecies and the meaning of the Long Count was that the Mayans were at one and the same time talking about potential future events and at the same time talking of stages of consciousness. He argued that at this watershed, if we successfully survive the transition, we would then enter a sixth world of consciousness. I'd agree and have in various books with the idea that we are entering a new stage of consciousness, though I would hardly dare to date it as exactly as the twentytwelveologists have, or even to pick a particular year. Major changes in consciousness, whether in a person or a culture, normally take place so subtly that we don't realize that they have taken place until long after the fact.

SYMBOLS AND SIGNS

Prophecies are symbolic. Unfortunately few in our materialistic times understand symbolism. We want something to be either true or false, with no shadings in between. We especially don't understand that something can be psychologically and spiritually true without being in any way literally true. In the Western World, for example, too often we try and take a symbolic document, like the Bible, literally. That leads to two ridiculous extremes:

- the scientist who condemns the Bible out of hand as nonsense because he knows that the world wasn't created in seven actual days, nor is it only 4,000 years old; or
- the fundamentalist who accepts everything in the Bible as literally true even if it contradicts known historical or scientific facts. As a little girl, my mother heard a minister in her Southern town say: "I believe in everything the Bible says. If the Bible said that Jonah swallowed the whale, I'd believe it."

The great religious works are records left by someone who had a powerful mystical vision into the heights and the depths of the spirit. Mystical visions are impossible to communicate rationally, since there are no words adequate for the experience. However, since visionaries feel compelled to make an attempt at communication, they are forced to express the inexpressible in the only language possible: symbolism. The symbol system they use is normally common to their particular culture. That is, a Jewish mystic will communicate a vision in terms of

Jewish religious symbolism; a Hopi or Mayan shaman will communicate his vision in terms of Hopi/Mayan religious symbolism.

Jung said that a living symbol is the "best possible expression for what is still unknown." (18) Consider Jung's statement as a hypothesis in dealing with both the Hopi/Mayan prophesies as well as Western prophesies, such as those in the Book of Revelation of the Christian bible. Jung meant that a symbol cannot be reduced to any simple definition because it is prior to definition. Symbols come first, rational explanations come much, much later. As Jung never tired of stressing, a symbol is not a sign.

Though Jewish, Christian, Hindu, Muslim and Hopi mystics express their individual visions in symbolism characteristic of their cultures, the actual experience tends to be largely identical. Therefore, once the cultural trappings are removed or translated, the underlying symbolism is universal. That's why, for example, a conscious pastiche using symbols reduced to signs (which was a common literary form in the Middle Ages) no longer engages our interest, while a true vision using seemingly identical symbolism still captivates us.

We all encounter similar symbols every night in our dreams. Both Freud and Jung realized that dreams, coming from the unconscious, are pre-verbal and speak not in words, but in symbols. But Freud regarded symbols largely as empty signs: long objects are phallic symbols, hollow objects symbols of the vagina. In contrast, Jung regarded dreams as sacred mysteries, each a window on both our personal unconscious and on a transpersonal realm he termed the collective unconscious.

Jung argued that a true symbol is inexhaustible. As an example, a cave in a dream might, in part, represent a woman's vagina. It might represent anything hidden away from consciousness. The symbol of a cave would carry all the connotations that caves have had both in our personal life and in the life of mankind. We might have visited one of the great caves, like the Carlsbad Caverns or Mammoth Caverns. We might remember Tom Sawyer's harrowing adventure in the cave with Injun Joe. We might remember the Caves of Mirrabar in *Passage to India*. Each such experience of a cave would impart a particular resonance to our approach to caves.

Hundreds of thousands of years ago, our ancestors lived in caves, protected against the terrors of the night. Tens of thousands of years ago, their first religious ceremonies were held in special caves, hidden from the knowledge of those not allowed into their mysteries. Two thousand years ago, the ancestors of many of us buried their dead in catacombs, holy places where at least in death they could be safe from persecution.

When we dream of a cave, all of those associations cluster around the symbol of a cave. The similarities and differences between our particular dream cave and all those other associated caves further color the symbol. The context in which the cave occurs in the dream, the dreams we have had before in which caves appear, everything adds to the richness of the symbol. It is just not sufficient to reduce a cave in a dream to a vagina.

For Jung, every person, every object, every situation in a dream is a symbol, capable of almost infinite amplification; i.e., we don't follow a single associational string of memories back to a single source, nor do we say a cave equals a vagina and that's that. Instead, we build up a penumbra of associations, personal and transpersonal, that surround every part of the dream. The associations between each person, each object, each situation in the dream blur into each other since ultimately every symbol can encompass all of man's experience, if it's stretched far enough.

Let's return to Jung's contention that a symbol is the "best possible expression for what is still unknown." In our example, a cave occurs in a dream because there is something unknown which is being presented to our conscious minds from the unconscious, something for which we have no adequate verbal expression. This unknown something can be better expressed by a cave, a particular cave in a particular circumstance, than by anything else. Once we consciously understand the issue presented by the dream, it's no longer unknown; the unconscious no longer needs to show us that particular cave.

THE COLLECTIVE UNCONSCIOUS

What is the source of these symbols which appear in the Hopi prophecies, in great religious works, in our daily dreams? In his studies of the dreams and fantasies of his patients, as well as in his readings of the mythologies of widely divergent cultures, Jung came to accept that each of us contains within us a doorway into a far wider world which he called the collective unconscious: "collective" because it is accessible to all, "unconscious" because it can't be reached through conscious awareness. It's a much maligned and much more misunderstood concept. Material which emerges from the collective unconscious has a vast amount of emotional energy; it is experienced as numinous, awesome, eerie, godlike, or any of the other human reactions to the more-than-human.

The great religious historian Mircea Eliade saw the world of myths and prophesies much as did Jung, but with a difference in emphasis. The great moments in the life of a person or a nation are all existential crises, times when no solution based solely on reason or tradition will do. These watersheds generate incredible energy because of our nearly total involvement in the issue, our inability to escape from the problem. At such times, this energy enables us to transcend our normal world and pass into the world of religion; we are forced by our desperate need to advance into a new relationship with divinity. Eliade sees religion as coming into existence at the "limit points" of human experience.

Eliade sees the world of the collective unconscious accessible to the individual through dreams and visions as only one manifestation of the Godhead, and a limited one if it isn't actualized in the outer world. Thus Eliade sees the myth as more primary than the dream, because it was powerful enough to move many men, not just one as the vision or dream of an individual might. Jung sees the dream as foremost, the myth its best attempt at collective expression. But both are far too aware of just how difficult it is to denote primacy to either inside or outside, individual or collective, when the gods play with the world.

BEYOND LINEARITY

Once we begin to think symbolically, we begin to live symbolically. We reject literal interpretation, we reject linearity. As I've mentioned earlier in this chapter, the Hopis' great migrations consisted of moving as far as they could go in one direction, then returning to their starting place, making a cycle or a round: thus circularity.

Returning to the starting point, they turned at right angles and made another "round." Four "rounds" made a cross, seemingly linear. Yet there was more; at the end of each arm of the cross, the Hopis took care to turn briefly at right angles before they retraced their path; thus the cross really formed a swastika. A swastika is an expression of the movement inherent in the seemingly linear; a swastika is ready to spin, forming a wheel. If the above seems to the reader to be far too complex for supposedly "primitive" natives to understand, I can assure him otherwise. The Hopis are totally aware of all the symbolism I've mentioned above and have refined it at great lengths in their elaborate symbol system.

> From one point of view the unconscious is a purely natural process without design, but from another it has that potential directed-ness which is characteristic of all energy processes. When the conscious mind participates actively and experiences each stage of the process, or at least understands it intuitively, then the next image always starts off on the higher level that has been won, and purposiveness develops. [19]

At a very difficult time in his early adult life, four years after breaking with Sigmund Freud, Jung had a great dream which showed him that the developmental path each of us takes during his or her life (which Jung termed "individuation") is not linear. Instead, it could be best expressed by a spiral. A spiral is both cyclical and linear, thus much like the Hopis' swastika.

Visualize a spring resting on its base, coiling upward. Taking a godlike view, looking down on the spring from the sky, it looks like a single circle. Looked at from the ground, it appears like a series of sloping lines, each separate and distinct, advancing into the sky. From the godlike view, moving around the spiral is just an endless trip around the circle, each time coming back to the starting point in a rather Sisyphean effort. However, from the ground, the movement seems to pass gently upward, disappear for a moment, then appear at a higher level, ready to begin another upward journey.

PSYCHOLOGICAL CONTAINERS

The important thing in viewing any prophesy is to resist the temptation to become lost in a useless examination of its literal truth. It's fascinating if the Hopi, Mayan and Tibetan Buddhist prophesies actually predicted the critical world events leading up to our present watershed. But we are more concerned with symbolic truth than literal truth. The Hopi prophesies speak symbolic truths about changes in consciousness. Prophetic literature of all cultures speak in symbols, symbols whose primary purpose is to capture inner, not outer, change.

If the symbols are accurate enough to show outer events as well, more power to them. But prophesies are records of inner experiences of transformations and transcendence. These experiences are more similar than dissimilar, regardless of the time, place, or individual identity of the person recording them. Thus all are potentially available to serve as psychological "containers" during times of struggle and transformation.

Therefore, in a time of major transition, a time like today, we can approach such prophetic literature as potential "containers" for our own new vision of reality. This vision seems too strange to be directly perceivable; it has to be seen through symbolic lenses. We need to find images, stories, songs, poems, that awaken something both old and new inside us. We need symbols that capture something of this strange new time, so that we have some alternative to the endless litanies of gloom and despair. The new is frightening because it destroys the old. But the new is also a thing in itself, and needs to be seen as such, not merely as the destroyer of the old, the negation of the known.

As Mircea Eliade never tired of demonstrating in his writing, religion appears when something is differentiated from its environment and labeled as holy. In Eliade's terms, prophetic visions are holy because we have singled them out as holy. One sure sign of this holiness is that such visions never lose their magic power to arouse strong emotions; though we can read many contradictory meanings into their words, the words continue to fascinate. In fact, it is exactly because we can read multiple meanings into the words and images that they continue to fascinate us. All true myths and prophesies contain that more-than-human allotment of energy; they fascinate at a level not accessible to logical analysis. I hope that readers, like the Hopis, can realize that prophesies speak more to the spirit than the flesh.

When something eternal in the human psyche speaks to us, the vehicle is not important. The only question is whether we can still experience the mystery of the revelation. If we come to prophetic material with the right attitude, we feel a chill run up our spine. Something deep inside us can still experience symbols directly, without the need for intellectual interpretation. And, if prophetic material is psychologically true, questions of literal truth or falsity are immaterial. When we approach the Hopis' teachings or the Mayan prophesies (or the Book of Revelation), we need to listen with our whole being. The chill of recognition is important because these prophesies offer not only an end, but also a new beginning.

[This article was adapted from material in Robin Robertson, *At the End of Time* (Nicolas-Hays, 2011).]

REFERENCES

1. Frank Waters, *Book of the Hopi* (New York: Penguin, 1977), p. xi. First published in 1963.

2. Frank Waters, *Book of the Hopi*, p. 104.

3. Frank Waters, *Book of the Hopi*, p. 115.

4. Frank Waters, *Book of the Hopi*, p. 127.

5. Frank Waters, *Book of the Hopi*, p. 131.

6. From the radio interview of John Kimmey, by Michael Toms, New Dimension Radio, Tape #1741, 1987.

7. This and the following quotes are from the John Kimmey interview.

8. *See Frank Waters,* Mexico Mystique: the Coming Sixth World of Consciousness *(Chicago: Save Books, 1975).*

9. This and previous quote from William Wordsworth, "The Prelude, Book Sixth: Cambridge and the Alps." Retrieved Sept. 23, 2010, from Bartleby.com, http://www.bartleby.com/145/ww292.html.

10. John D. Barrow, *The Book of Nothing* (New York: Vintage Books, Random House, 2000), pp. 27-28.

11. See a history of the complex issue of the discovery and evolution of zero in John D. Barrow, *The Book of Nothing*, chapter. 1.

12. Frank Waters, *Mexico Mystique*, p. 252.

13. Frank Waters, *Mexico Mystique*, p. 250.

14. John Major Jenkins, "The Origin of the 2012 Revolution," in *The Mystery of 2012* (Boulder, CO: Sounds True, 2009), pp. 37-66.

15. AP article, Mexico City, Oct. 12, 2009. Retrieved Oct. 5, 2010, from http://www.cbsnews.com/stories/2009/10/12/ap/strange/main5378465.shtml.

16. Also from AP article, Mexico City, Oct. 12, 2009. Retrieved Oct. 5, 2010, from http://www.cbsnews.com/stories/2009/10/12/ap/strange/main5378465.shtml.

17. John Major Jenkins, *The 2012 Story* (New York: Tarcher/Penguin, 2009), pp. 96-97.

18. C. G. Jung, *CW6: Psychological Types* (Princeton: Princeton University Press, 1971/1976), par. 820.

19. C. G. Jung, CW7: *Two Essays on Analytical Psychology* (Princeton: Princeton University Press, 1966), par. 386.

INNER VOICES

The Shadow & Other Inner Personalities

Some of the same considerations apply to this inner relationship as to relationships between people in the outer world. For example, full regard for the other's separateness and idiosyncracies is essential. In the inner relationship, the unconscious must be permitted to be what it is, and not forced into ego or external notions of how it ought to behave. At the same time, the ego must hold firmly to its own reality. This is as difficult in inner as in outer relationships.

Janet Dallet. (1)

There are not one but many shadows within us. Or perhaps it would be better to say that the shadow takes many forms. In early dreams, the shadow may take the form of a vampire or a werewolf, an alien or even an animal. This is because at this early stage, the shadow seems so strange and unrecognizable that only such distorted images will do. But it's not as if we dream of a werewolf, and then that same werewolf keeps popping up in dream after dream. Instead, a variety of such images occur, not only in the early stages of dealing with the shadow, but throughout your dream life. The shadow figures form in the unconscious around the issues that have emotional significance for you. Jungian analyst John Talley has commented that: "There are many, probably as many shadows as there are entities or affects." Over time, different figures come into existence, transform, melt into one another, disappear, reappear, and eventually merge into consciousness.

A Portrait of the Psyche's Structure: Multiple Personalities

> . . . *in* multiple personality, the skeletal structure of the psyche is laid bare. *A window is opened into the soul, and the structure and dynamics of its "internal organs" can be observed in a vividly direct way. The theoretical and practical importance of the phenomenon of multiple personality for understanding the human psych cannot be minimized.*
>
> Richard Noll. (2)

One can see these inner figures most clearly in cases of Multiple Personality Disorder (MPD). The unfortunate people suffering from MPD have normally had such traumatic backgrounds in their childhood that they have never developed a single stable central personality (i.e., an ego). For most of us, our birth personality evolves over time, from a tiny sense of personal identity into a single all-encompassing ego which forms the center of all of our conscious personality. The shadow appears in order to break up that monolithic structure so that we can add parts of the unconscious into a new structure.

The designation of MPD has been replaced by DID (Dissociative Identity Disorder) by the American Psychological Association. I find the original description better describes the condition as I've experienced it with patients.

For MPD patients, their birth personality may or may not have survived as the main conscious personality, but one or more (usually many more) other personalities have formed as well. Under varying situations, one of these personalities takes control of consciousness. When this happens, the new personality can be as different from the old as any two people are. The normal conscious personality usually remains unaware of these alternate personalities. Because of this, MPD sufferers become experts at rationalizing to themselves gaps in their memory. It is fascinating that often one of the alternate personalities does have full memory of everything that has taken place, no matter which personality was in charge.

It's easy to see why it would be invaluable for alternate personalities to appear in someone who has an especially troubling childhood. When their situation becomes too unbearable, the child simply withdraws from conscious awareness of what is happening and lets another personality take over, one who is better able to deal with the situation. Once considered so rare a malady that many psychologists denied that it even existed, in recent years MPD has become increasingly prevalent. This parallels the growth in related phenomena among healthy personalities, such as channeling (of which, more below). The reasons for this are complex and highly debatable and not central to our discussion here. My own guess is that this is one of many signs that the collective unconscious is rising, preparatory to a major change in consciousness.

After one of my earlier books was published, which discussed MPD, I had quite a number of MPD patients contact me either by letter or e-mail. They felt "seen" by me in a way that they hadn't by most therapists. I worked briefly with a few of them, and for more than a year with one patient, who I'll call Suzanne. What surprised me was that we were able to do our work together exclusively through e-mail! All I needed to do was put the name of the personality I wanted to talk to in the header of the e-mail and that was the only personality that read and answered the e-mail. Suzanne was an artist who had been able to function successfully in the outer world despite having MPD. The biggest problem she had was that incessantly throughout the day she would hear a little girl's voice in her mind saying: "I'll be good, Daddy. Please don't hurt me." Over and over and over.

Much of my work was with the little girl, who I'll call Mary. She was pre-school age, perhaps 5 or 6, but she could read and write, at least at a primitive level. She didn't want to talk about her Daddy, who was actually long dead in real life. So instead I sent her pictures and asked her to tell me what she saw in the pictures. This process helped enough that Suzanne didn't hear Mary's voice quite so incessantly, but the pleas didn't go away totally.

After working with Suzanne and Mary (and other personalities less frequently), I decided that I had to confront the father. Though he was dead, I realized that he was as alive inside Suzanne's and Mary's shared psyche as when he was alive in the outer world. So I sent an e-mail, asking him to talk with me. He did answer, as if he had no choice, but he was protean, slipping away from any attempt to pin him down. He was as nasty a person as I've ever encountered, but I finally managed to get him to agree to stop hurting little Mary. At that point, Mary's incessant pleas ceased inside Suzanne, though Mary was still alive as a sub-personality. I was never able to fully integrate the personalities, but life was better for Suzanne than it was before. Soon after this we broke off our work, as we both knew this was as much as we were going to be able to do together.

I'll just mention one more thing that struck me as odd during that time when I was being contacted by a variety of people with MPD: I found that there were MPD wannabes. Yes, there are people who want to believe that they have multiple personalities, even though they don't. I had no trouble at all distinguishing people who actually had MPD from those who just wanted to have it. Years later I saw a documentary about Kenneth Bianchi, who raped and murdered women along with his cousin Angelo Buono. Bianchi claimed he was innocent because he suffered from MPD and an alternate personality committed the crimes. The documentary included video showing Bianchi being interviewed by a psychiatrist who bought his story hook-line-and-sinker. I was shocked as he was so obviously not an MPD that I couldn't believe he could fool anyone. He obviously had studied some textbook descriptions of multiple personality patients and copied them, but there was no depth to his portrayal.

Myers, Flournoy and the Creative Unconscious

Between our ordinary consciousness (the supraliminal) and our latent consciousness (the subliminal) there are perpetual changes and fluctuations along their border; the level of separation is not constant; the partition is not impervious; the threshold is not fixed between these parts of our being.

Théodore Flournoy. (3)

Though virtually all the literature on MPD treats it as exclusively a pathological condition, a view that traces itself back to the prominent French psychologist, Pierre

Janet, Jung took a different stance. He felt that the psyche inherently organized emotional issues into *complexes,* which then inevitably took personified form. All change in the psyche takes place through the formation of such inner figures and the conscious ego's engagement with them through dreams and fantasies. Without taking a personified form, there is virtually no way for consciousness to confront these issues. For Jung, this was a natural and essentially benign function of the psyche. As he says: "Consciousness is continually widened through the confrontation with previously unconscious contents, or--to be more accurate--could be widened if it took the trouble to integrate them." (4) In other words, Jung is saying that we all have such inner figures, and that their formation in the unconscious is a necessary first step toward integration into our personality.

Though Jung didn't explicitly acknowledge the debt, he was drawing on ideas first expressed by a mentor, Swiss psychologist Théodore Flournoy, who had befriended Jung during the critical period when Jung was splitting from Freud. Flournoy in turn was drawing on the work of Frederick Myers, a pioneer in parapsychological research. Myers had developed a theory of the unconscious -which he called the *subliminal*-based on his study of phenomena which existed on the border between conscious and unconscious, especially *automatic writing*. Automatic writing is what it sounds like: letting writing come out of yourself on its own, automatically, with no conscious intervention. This can be done in any way from using a Ouija board to point to letters, to holding a pen or pencil in your hand and letting your hand write seemingly on its own, to sitting at a typewriter or computer keyboard and allowing the words to flow. As we will see later in our discussion of Jung's technique of Active Imagination, this process is surprisingly easy.

One of Myers first discoveries was the ease with which information flowed during automatic writing. Over one hundred thousand books of such writing have been "self-published or published by vanity presses . . . in the United States over the last hundred years." Myers found that there was no evidence that the ability to channel such writing was an indication of a pathological condition. He found the unconscious which produced the writing of more interest.

> The subwaking self is devoid of all personal characteristics, it is both personal and impersonal . . . it assumes indifferently all kinds of character and of person, for it has no individuality. (5)

In contrast to those who viewed such unconscious processes as pathological and at best subservient to consciousness, Myers found that *"the unconscious mentation flowed on intercurrently with the conscious."* This is a very important statement. In the 1930's, brain physiologist Dr. Wilder Penfield found that electric stimulation to various parts of the brain could reproduce memories as vivid as if the person was experiencing them for the first time. He thought that proved that consciousness was just a byproduct of the brain. In 1959, however, while a patient's brain was being electrically stimulated such that he was experiencing childhood memories, *at the same time he was consciously aware of what was going on in the room where the experiment was taking place.* Hence two separate and distinct streams of consciousness were going on at the same time!

Channeling Zenon: Confusing the Container with the Contained

There remains one last question to pose concerning these new forms of psychological existence. Are they inferior or superior to the waking state?

Pierre Janet. (6)

In October of 1988, I had a personal experience with a channel that caused me to think deeply about the nature of channeling. I had been reading Jane Roberts' books for the first time. Though I had never had any particular interest in her books before, for some reason I read one of the more personal books, which was filled with Jane Roberts' speculations about her experience of Seth. I found it fascinating. When I tried the Seth books themselves, I didn't find them particularly interesting, but all of Jane Roberts' books about her own quest for knowledge were compelling because she was struggling with much the same issues I struggled with in coming to integrate the shadow into my life.

In search of more of Jane Roberts' books, I went to a local new age bookstore. When I paid for the books at the counter, the salesperson asked if I was interested in channels. When I said that I was, he mentioned that he hadn't found many good channels, but he did know of one good one. Would I be interested? I was, so he gave me the name and phone number of the man who channeled an entity we'll call Zenon. I contacted the man-we'll say his name was Ted--and arranged to come to a weekly class which Zenon taught.

The first (and last) session was a real experience. I never got quite straight what exactly Zenon was supposed to be. This class had been going on for quite a while, so everyone but me already knew everything about Zenon. I think he claimed to be some being who lived in many time and space dimensions at the same time, but it is really not significant; whatever his claimed origins, Zenon was a trip! The topic of the class I attended was "guilt." Basically Zenon said that all emotions are only energy patterns and guilt is a useless waste of energy. There was never any situation in which guilt had any positive purpose. Something like that. This was overstated, but was clearly a useful thing for most of those attending to hear. More interesting than the speech was Zenon's ability to manipulate energy.

Ted, an ex-lawyer (at least he said he was an ex-lawyer) made his living now as a "psychic counselor." While trying his best to look the part of the mystic seer, Ted was basically a quiet, subdued person with a fair amount of rather typical occult knowledge. No, Ted wasn't anything special; we have all seen lot of Teds. Zenon, on the other hand, exuded power. At one point, when Zenon had been saying that emotions were merely energy and totally under our control, one young woman said that she had no control over her emotions and didn't understand what he meant by saying emotions were energy. Zenon then did some "tricks" with energy. He turned his forefingers in tiny circles around each other in front of the young woman. She found herself getting very confused. Then he stopped the movement and commanded her to "stop." She was clear again. The men on each side of her also got confused. I was far enough away that I only felt a funny tingling sensation. Zenon then raised and lowered the energy in the room. When he turned his hands palm up and raised them, we all felt full of energy. When he turned them palm down and lowered them, the energy drained away again.

Several times during the evening, when he sensed the energy level dropping, he raised it again. I experienced this as clearly as if he were turning on a faucet. In fact, I would say that I felt the energy to a greater degree than the others. After the class, everyone had a little potluck snack. I talked with Ted and his wife, telling them how excited I was about Zenon's use of energy. I told how I had done something similar, though much simpler, in working with schizophrenic patients. They both gave me some funny looks; I was clearly not their typical student. When I got home and excitedly told my wife about the evening, she said that she could feel energy coming from me as I walked in the door.

The next week, I came at the time I had thought we were supposed to arrive, but which turned out to be a half an hour early. I went directly up to their apartment and rang the bell. There were sounds like Ted and his wife were quarreling, which stopped when I rang the bell. Ted came to the door and said rudely: "You're early, come back in a half hour." I went outside and waited as others arrived. After a while, I went upstairs again with two of the women. Ted opened the door and graciously greeted the two women with hugs and kisses and kind words. He asked me to wait a minute, then closed the door on me. He came back a few minutes later and angrily handed me the $75 I had paid for five sessions. He said: "I don't like your vibes. I don't want you here. Here's your money back." I was shocked and said for want of anything else: "You should at least take $15 for the session I attended." He took $15 and then closed the door on me, nearly slamming it. I was shocked.

All the way home, I examined my actions to see if I had done something offensive, if I had given cause for being accused of having "bad vibes." After I thought it over, I felt sure it was Ted who had the problem, not me. I thought about his reaction to me, both the previous week and this week at the door. After piecing together little hints, I was surprised to realize that Ted was afraid of me; I was outside his experience and it frightened him. What a laugh! A something or other of incredible power was talking through him and he was afraid of me.

That made me start thinking more about the nature of channeling. Reading Jane Roberts, I had found Seth a mite boring, but Jane herself fascinating. It was just the opposite with Ted and Zenon. Ted was a person of pretty average abilities, and probably a little screwed up, as was evidenced by his reaction to me. But Zenon was someone with incredible power, much more power than I sensed even quiescent in Ted. Where did those abilities come?

Remember Frederick Myers statement that "the subwaking self is devoid of all personal characteristics, it is both personal and impersonal . . . it assumes indifferently all kinds of character and of person, for it has no individuality." It's all well and good to accept such possibilities abstractly; it is something else again when you experience the power of a personality such as Zenon, as I did. As we will see later, it is still another level to experience such a personality within yourself.

Channeling Jung: Is Nothing Sacred?

If we are multiplex beings, let us get the advantage of our multiplicity.

Frederick Myers. (7)

Nearly two years later, I had an experience with another channel, though at one remove. I came home one Friday evening and found an intriguing message on my answering machine. A man with a strong Germanic accent said that his wife channeled C. G. Jung. He had brought a videocassette of a session which had been shown on Swiss TV. He had already shown the video at the Los Angeles Jung Institute. Someone there had given him my name as a person who might be interested. Since he had to leave Los Angeles the next day, he asked if I might want to see him that evening. How could I turn down such an intriguing invitation? Reading between the lines, I guessed that his reception at the Jung Institute had been less than enthusiastic and he was hoping to find someone who was more receptive.

On the phone, Rene had sounded like a man in his '60s. I imagine I was thrown off because of the accent, because the man I met looked like a man in his early '30s (though he actually turned out to be 40). He was charming and open as he told me a series of incredible events that had led him first to meet his wife, Mirabelle, then for her to become a channel, first for their unborn son, then for Jung. The video of Mirabelle channeling Jung was fascinating. She sat wrapped in a blanket, flanked by Rene on her left and a very proper Swiss male interviewer on her right. She went into trance easily and Rene opened the evening for questions from the interviewer. The interviewer was careful to ask his questions of Jung, and sober questions they were. The interview went on for nearly an hour until Jung (sic) indicated it was time to bring the interview to an end.

Later when Rene and I talked about all this, he told me that Mirabelle was a "conscious channel;" i.e., she was aware of everything Jung said as she channeled it. Jung had insisted on that, Rene told me; Jung said he had previously been channeled through unconscious mediums and found the experience unsatisfactory. This was very significant to me. When Jane Roberts channeled Seth, she was described as becoming a different person with a different voice, personality, etc. When Ted channeled Zenon in my presence, it was like a totally different personality of immense power had entered the room. In contrast, when Mirabelle channeled Jung, her voice remained the voice of a young woman.

She spoke slowly, her face sometimes twisting slightly with effort, as if she were concentrating to read something on an inner screen that was difficult to see or translating words that she could barely hear. There was little rise or fall in the pitch of her voice, and the pauses had nothing to do with the material delivered. It was more like she paused when she needed breath, even though that might be in the middle of a paragraph or even a sentence. I couldn't imagine someone consciously dictating that way without an inordinate amount of practice. The material itself was a strange amalgamation of Jungian thought, coupled with a sort of generic new age channeled philosophy which is heard over and over, especially in the second-rate channels. Freudian terms like "regression," which are used rarely in Jung's writing, were used extensively. Yet, interestingly enough, the philosophy expressed was largely Jungian. One of the most fascinating examples occurred early in the interview. When the interviewer asked Jung what he thought of being televised, Jung, instead of answering directly, used film and projection as a metaphor which he extended to great lengths in a general discussion of the nature of reality. The ideas expressed in this lengthy metaphor, while totally in line with Jung's ideas and beautifully developed in a way that I have never seen expressed anywhere in his collected works, were presented in a manner which was totally different from Jung's normal manner of presentation.

Still further from the Jung of his writings was the channeled Jung's explicit acceptance of positions he dismissed in his writings; e.g. the channeled Jung accepted reincarnation literally. However, he was far less explicit in answer to a question as to whether he was the same Jung we had known as a living entity. There he gave a brilliant answer that would not have been unworthy of Jung. The whole interview was a mixture of such likely and unlikely, pedestrian and inspired comments. It certainly wasn't Jung as I know him through his writings and through the films of him I've seen, but there was material Jung would not have been unproud of, original material. Of special interest in this context, Rene told me afterwards that neither he nor Mirabelle had read any of Jung prior to Mirabelle channeling Jung. As with Jane Roberts and Seth, the channeling had gone on for a while before Jung identified himself as Jung.

This is the kind of thing you either have to dismiss as fraud (and there has been plenty of fraud in the history of both spiritualist mediums and modern channels), or you have to accept that somehow people who know little or nothing about Jung are able to channel information that fits Jung. I assumed the truth of Rene's statement, first because he seemed a truthful (even innocent) sort of person. Second, he was definitely not a bookish type nor, from what he said of Mirabelle, did she seem the type to have dug deeply into Jung. And, of course, if they had, Mirabelle would hardly have had so many non-Jungian phrases in the channeling. Third, if Rene and Mirabelle were phonies who had just learned a few simple catch phrases of Jungian psychology, that would explain the strange mixture of Jungian and Freudian language. But then how to explain the extreme complexity and subtlety of some of the explanations? No, I'm afraid that denying the honesty of the channeling process leads to more, not less, complex explanations.

One is forced to accept that we have access to information inside us which is capable of transcending our normal conscious abilities (remember Jung's transcendent function?). But that inner voice (or voices) is also capable of delivering drivel that we would never accept consciously, unless we thought it was coming from some higher power independent of us. We can set aside our conscious personality totally and let the inner voices have full control, as Jane Roberts did with Seth, and Ted did with Zenon, or we can share consciousness, as Mirabelle did with Jung.

Eileen Garrett: Who Speaks to a Medium?

Eileen Garrett was probably the most famous medium of the 20th century, and one who worked extensively with scientists who studied her varied abilities. As part of that collaboration, she approached Ira Progoff, asking him to interview the spirit guides she used in her psychic readings. She knew that the two standard explanations were that the entities speaking through a medium were either actual people who had lived before, or parts of her own personality. Neither explanation seemed sufficient to her.

Progoff interviewed four separate spirit guides that Garrett used. He recorded the results of these interviews in a remarkable book: *The Image of an Oracle.* Two of the spirit guides were supposedly dead humans: one a 13th century Arab soldier, the other a 17th century Persian physician. The other two were self-described as gods. Progoff reminds the reader that:

> The phenomena that occur, the voices, the persons, the imagery, are such that we are not at all entitled to assume that they are what they appear to be. On the contrary, they are symbolic expressions. They are symbolic representations of dimensions of human experience that cannot be fitted into our ordinary categories of knowledge. (8)

When Progoff tried to find out from the spirit guides whether they were actual persons or parts of Mrs. Garrett's personality, their answers were complex. He decided that they were best thought of as "symbolic forms of dramatization by which larger principles of life are made articulate in human experience and by which our intimations of meaning in life are made more specific."

Dr. Henry Reed, famed for his work with dreams as well as other areas, interpreted Progoff's findings this way:

> Progoff learns that questioning them about their *identity* is inappropriate. They cannot give a meaningful answer to an inappropriate question without falsifying the whole topic. . . . Furthermore, he learns that these spirits are intimately connected to Mrs. Garrett herself, and to get rid of them would be to get rid of her, and vice versa. He learns that rather than ask *who* is speaking . . . it would be better to ask *what quality of consciousness* or level of reality is being expressed at the moment. . . .Rather than think of these spirits as persons, or sub-personalities, therefore, Progoff concludes that it's more accurate to think of them as *personifications.* [(9)]

It will be well to keep this complexity in mind in all our dealings with the shadow in his many manifestations, and especially in Active Imagination, which is our final topic.

Active Imagination: Talking with the Shadow

The greatest use of active imagination really is to put us--like the rainmaker--into harmony with the Tao so that the right things may happen around us instead of the wrong.

Barbara Hannah. [(10)]

Barbara Hannah was one of the first Jungian analysts, as well as a biographer of Jung. The "rainmaker" she mentions is from a story Jung loved to tell, one which he told her to be sure to use whenever she gave a lecture or seminar on Jungian psychology. Jung said that his friend Richard Wilhelm-the translator of the I Ching and The Secret of the Golden Flower-told him the story was a personal experience with a Chinese rainmaker.

Wilhelm was visiting a village devastated by a drought. In desperation, the villagers sent for a rainmaker. When the rainmaker arrived, he asked to be provided with a small hut at the edge of the village where he could live. He then went into the hut and didn't emerge again for three days. The next day it not only rained, it began to snow, to the delight of the villagers. While the people of the village scampered in delight, Wilhelm asked the priest how he had brought the rain. The priest said that when he came to the village, he could feel that it was "out of the Tao;" that is, emotionally disturbed, uncentered. That made him feel "out of the Tao" as well. So he withdrew to the hut until he was once more "in Tao." When he did so, the snow came.

The shadow appears in our life when we are out of the Tao. Our conscious ego position no longer qualifies as a center. Instead we are pulled between its values and a new set of unconscious values which form around the shadow. Those values become personified and appear in our dreams. To the extent we make an attempt to remember those dreams, to record them, and to try and engage with them (I won't say try to figure out what they mean because that is less important), we begin a dialogue with the unconscious which can eventually reconcile us with the shadow. But there is another way: *Active Imagination*.

In the introduction to her excellent collection of Jung's writings on active imagination, *Jung on Active Imagination*, Joan Chodorow pointed out that Jung gave this tool any number of different names before he settled on "active imagination." At first it was the "transcendent function." Later he called it the "picture method." Other names were "active fantasy" and "active phantasying." Sometimes the process was referred to as "trancing," "visioning," "exercises," "dialectical method," "technique of differentiation," "technique of introversion," "introspection," and "technique of the descent." (11)

These earlier terms are useful in that they call up different pictures in our mind of what the process can be. Whatever term is used, active imagination is the process of consciously dialoguing with our unconscious. There are many ways to do this, and anyone who begins the process eventually tries many methods. But two in particular, which we might call the visual and the oral, are useful. In either case, one should ritualize the process in some way in order to set it off from normal life. This is important because essentially you are going to go into an altered state of consciousness, one which will be unique to your particular version of active imagination.

At least initially, you should establish some ritual of your own for doing active imagination. You can retire to a special room, dim the lights, relax, anything that feels right for you. One simple method is just to sit comfortably, close your eyes for a moment, take a deep breath, and let it out. Then move your awareness to different parts of your body; i.e., become aware of your feet, then perhaps your arms, then your head. After you can readily move your awareness anywhere in your body, open your eyes and begin an active imagination.

Use something previously produced by the unconscious as a starting point; for example, a shadow dream in which you were present. In the visual technique, allow yourself to drift back into the setting of the dream until you can see it in your mind. Then allow the dream to grow and develop, except that now instead of the dream determining your actions, you determine your own actions. You shouldn't try to control the dream itself-you'll find that impossible anyway-but only how you act in the dream.

You should try to behave in a manner which would be appropriate if the dream were actually happening. In a dream, if your behavior is inappropriate to the situation, it is an indication that this is an issue you are not dealing with yet in your life. For example, if someone you care about is threatened in a dream, yet you observe it dispassionately, something is normally amiss. (I say normally because there are no absolutes in dealing with the unconscious; for any rule I might make, I could find exceptions.) Of course, your sense of appropriate or inappropriate may change as you progress in acknowledging the shadow's right to its values. In an active imagination, you have the possibility of pushing yourself toward appropriate behavior that might take much longer to happen if you left the issue to dreams, or to actually evidence itself in real life through projection. (12)

Afterwards (or even during the active imagination), you should record what transpired so that you can review it later, just as you would a dream. You can do this with a tape recorder or at a computer keyboard, if that doesn't distract you, or simply with paper and pencil. If you use a tape recorder, you should later transcribe it into a written form.

Before we move on to the oral method, I want to stress that every single detail that I've mentioned above in discussing the visual technique might be untrue in your particular case. One of the primary reasons why some people do active imagination visually and some orally is that they vary in their major inner representational systems; i.e., some can visualize almost anything quite readily, others almost not at all. Some can readily hold a dialog in their mind, others find this impossible. Still others (and I'm one of those), are primarily kinesthetic; i.e., we feel things in our body. I'm not good at visualizing, and I don't normally talk things over in my head either. Instead my body feels whether something is right or wrong, and subtle body reactions determine how I interact with others. Since most of us assume that everyone must experience reality the same way that we do, these differences in representational systems can cause extreme difficulties in communication. Unfortunately, most systems that teach methods to induce and enhance altered states of consciousness are unaware of these differences and normally presume a visual orientation. Some Jungians, for example, actually presume that the visual method is superior to other methods (largely because that is the method used by Jung himself). But that's not the case; for Jung, the raison d'etre for active imagination is a way par excellence to "distinguish ourselves from the unconscious contents" of the psyche. And that can be done in any number of ways, not simply visually.

But even if you are visual, there are myriads of ways in which you may do active imagination. Jung was able to actually see fantasy characters in front of him, as if they were actually there. Joan Chodorow commented that "over time, he realized that when he managed to translate his emotions into images, he was inwardly calmed and reassured. He came to see that his task was to find the images that are concealed in the emotion." (13)

Those who are visual, but not to that extent, may simply close their eyes and see the fantasy unfold inside them as if it were a dream. Even if you might not be able to see the drama clearly, nevertheless, you will probably have an awareness of what is happening, which advances the action until once more you can see more clearly. There are many shadings possible.

In the oral technique, you hold a dialogue with a dream figure (or multiple dream figures), just as you would with someone in normal life. For example, you can pick a shadow figure who you found especially repulsive or frightening, and dialogue with it. You can actually do this out loud; if so, you may find Gestalt therapy techniques helpful at the beginning. For example, set two chairs facing each other. Sit in one and address the dream figure. Then move to the other chair, become the dream figure and see what you have to say. Move back-and-forth between the two chairs as you do this. You may feel foolish at first, but it takes very little time before that feeling goes away and the dialog becomes real. This is a technique originally developed by Fritz Perls, the founder of Gestalt therapy. Again there are many variations on this theme.

More prosaically (and probably more likely to be used by most of you), you can type at a computer keyboard or use a pad of paper and a pencil, to record a dialog as it goes on. If you are strongly oral, you may actually hear the dialog in your head as you go. If, like me, you are kinesthetic, you will more likely find that the dialog emerges without any intervening sounds inside your head. Since the representational systems often merge inside, these distinctions are not important and in no way should be considered to determine whether you are really having an active imagination or simply faking it (as is the opinion of the more skeptical of the psychologists who deal with hypnotism and other altered states of consciousness.)

What is important is that you give free rein, without editorializing, to what emerges from the unconscious. You take what it says seriously and answer as honestly as if you were dealing with a real person. The late Jungian analyst Janet Dallet stressed that: "Once the voice of the unconscious has been given form, the ego can confront it. It is only from this moment that we can legitimately speak of the process as active imagination, and it is only now that the personality can be deeply changed by it." (14)

This is the step that separates active imagination from channeling, such as we've discussed with Ted channeling Zenon and with Mirabelle's channeling of Jung. Ted and Zenon were two separate personalities, who merely shared time in inhabiting a single body. Perhaps Mirabelle may have gained from her channeling of Jung, since at least she was aware of what she was saying while she channeled Jung; yet still she never engaged actively with the Jung inside her. This need to hold up our own side of the discussion is important because the unconscious doesn't necessarily have all the answers. We have to be like Jacob in his struggle with the angel sent by God: willing to hold onto the strangers we encounter and neither accept nor reject their words blindly.

Though dreams are excellent sources of material for active imagination, they are not the only possibilities. You can take a mood, a fantasy element, anything emerging from your unconscious and use it as the beginning point for an active imagination. For example, once when I was experiencing a very profound sadness, I did an active imagination with my sadness. The sadness told me was that my heart chakra was opening up to another level, just as it did once before at a time when I was first seeing patients. Only this time, the higher chakras were opening up as well. That was why I was experiencing such pain. Knowing that my sadness had a meaning and a purpose made it feel holy; I stopped feeling like an animal in a trap. Life slowly started to once more become rich and complex.

This ability to talk to an emotion like sadness or anger is quite powerful. A man who attended one of my workshops was amazed at how easily he was able to do it. He said that he had spent thousands of dollars learning techniques to indirectly get at such emotional issues, "when all I had to do was talk to the emotion."

You can even construct a system in advance, in which the active imagination takes place. For example, many years ago, when I studied Western ceremonial magic, I learned a meditative system called "pathwalking" using the Kabalistic Tree of Life. The graphic representation of the Tree of Life has ten connection points (called sephiroth) connected by twenty-two paths. There is a complex system of associations-including colors, Tarot cards, etc.-for each sephiroth and path. One does path-walking by inducing an altered state (normal meditation is a good way to start), then selecting a particular sephiroth or path on the tree to enter (usually by envisioning a door you can open). Because of the web of associations you have already learned to each sephiroth and path, the unconscious has a rich fabric to work with in constructing a world you can then observe and interact with. As you walk different paths through this technique, they build up an intricate web of your own particular associations that ultimately define a Tree of Life unique to you. But note that this can be a merely passive exercise, if you are content to observe without interaction. It is the combination of observation of what the unconscious produces, plus conscious engagement that makes it active imagination.

As another example, psychologist Stephen Gallegos has a personally developed system involving animal imagery of power animals associated with each chakra. Jung felt that the land itself has a formative influence on the unconscious. Because of this all Americans have Native American symbols buried deep in our psyches. And power animals are embedded in the culture of many Native American tribes. I have had several indications from the unconscious in my dreams and dreams of patients, that it likes to use power animals as symbols, even explicit symbols for the chakras. For example, at a period when I felt under tremendous stress, I had a dream where I was driving down a deserted stretch of road. Up ahead I saw three wolves in the road. As I watched, to my delight, one of the wolves actually stood on his head.

Later, thinking about the dream, I decided that if the wolf was trying so hard to get my attention that he would stand on his head, I had better talk to him. So I did an active imagination with the wolf. He told me that he had appeared because it was time that he became my power animal (instead of the hawk who had been one for many years.) My problems came from being too much of a "lone wolf," and it was time for me to join the pack again. He stressed that I would not lose my individuality in the process, that every wolf, even though a member of a pack, was also an individual. Over the next several years, I made a conscious effort to fit in with the pack in several different settings. As I did so, though my life became even busier than before, the feeling of being under stress gradually declined. I was able to share responsibility with others, rather than feeling I had to always go it alone.

These more structured versions of active imagination are rarely mentioned by Jungians, and it is a shame that they aren't. One of the dangers of active imagination is that you can get in over your head much more readily than with dream work. The figures you encounter within active imagination are normally personified aspects of your own personality. As such, you can engage with them much as you would with people in outer life. But the shadow itself is only partially composed of undeveloped parts of your own personality; it has a collective aspect as well. It can connect with godlike (or demonic) energies that can overwhelm someone who is unprepared. Most often this takes the form of *inflation*; i.e., one literally gets puffed-up, inflated, with the energy. We assume that the more-than-human energies we are experiencing belong to us, that they are part of our own personality, and we ourselves are godlike. If the person's ego isn't secure, it is even possible to be possessed and induce a psychotic state. Jung says that sometimes "the subliminal contents already possess such a high energy that, when afforded an outlet by active imagination, they may overpower the conscious mind and take possession of the personality."

I used to see this often when I worked with more severely disturbed patients in a halfway home. Of course they were not doing active imagination; the unconscious came up without any instigation on their part. Usually they heard voices; they would talk about "good voices" and "bad voices," and normally knew which was which. But knowing which were good and which were bad voices didn't make them any easier to deal with. Sometimes the unconscious figures that produced the voices would rise to the surface of their own volition and take control. In one case, this was a demonic presence who told the patient to set fires, of which he had indeed set a string. Another would engage in a dialog with his voices, much as we've discussed for active imagination. Unfortunately, at such times, he was convinced the inner personality was an actual outer world person.

Possession is a very unlikely outcome unless one is already struggling to retain one's identity. To the extent that we "actively" (and I stress the "active") participate in our side of the exchange with the unconscious, even inflation is less likely to happen. Nevertheless, we will become inflated many times over the course of any system of spiritual development. Its equal-and-opposite counterpart is *depression,* again a literal description because the energy one normally has available is depressed, pushed down into the unconscious. The cycle of inflation and depression is inevitable if one opens a channel to the unconscious; the key is to recognize as soon as possible that we are becoming either inflated or depressed. Once we do, often the recognition itself is sufficient to center us once more. If not, it is effective to ground ourselves in the normal activities of life, especially those involving physical effort, or those which involve detail, which require our full attention.

I don't want to leave the reader with the impression that encountering more-than-human forces in the psyche is entirely negative. In the 5th century, Neoplatonist philosopher Proclus said that contemplative thought was not sufficient unto itself for enlightenment; it had to be coupled with *theurgy*. Theurgy was the ritual contacting of the gods, by allowing a particular god to possess us briefly. This is similar to religious rites in African and Pan-African religions such as Santería, Voodoo, Orisha, Lucumi, etc. In these traditions, many of these figures would qualify as personifications of the shadow, but a shadow grown so powerful that it has godlike powers. But they are honored and respected, rather than feared and reviled.

Theurgy "is based on the idea that, since the gods are the source of all, the nature of the gods is present, reflected hierarchically, in natural symbols and phenomena." (15) As with my path-walking exercises, someone like Proclus knew so many aspects of the Greek gods that he could go into an altered stated of consciousness and the archetypal energy of the god would flow through him.

Now Proclus was still too early in time to realize that the gods could be archetypal forces inside our psyches rather than physical beings. But we are psychological beings, aware that there is a world inside us as big as, or bigger than, the world outside us. When active imagination causes us to encounter collective personalities who are clearly separate from us, we are able to experience powers and abilities impossible in any other way. Though we must never fall into the trap of thinking that we are that godlike personality, just because it briefly flows through us, there is a part of every archetypal being that we can integrate into our own personality. This is not possible without actually experiencing the god, or the shadow.

If you do enough active imagination, you may eventually encounter a figure of profound wisdom and compassion. This is the figure Jung terms the Self. Here there is no need for fears about becoming inflated with the power we encounter; it is clearly not ours. Nor do we need to worry about mistrusting anything it might say to us. Sometimes we will first experience this power in a dream, when a voice tells us something, and we know it must be obeyed. The voice of the Self is unmistakable in a dream and equally unmistakable in active imagination. Once such a figure appears, you have a source of almost infinite wisdom available to help you during your development. Until it appears (and it may never), one should remember that the shadow, as distasteful as it seems, is our first presentiment of the Self.

Even those suffering from Multiple Personality Disorder often still have a connection to the Self through a "rational, usually all-knowing mature personality. . . . The inner self helper is sometimes a wise old man or teacher that claims to be chronologically older than the actual age of the patient." [16] When such a figure is present, it usually mitigates the more disastrous actions of other personalities. Once the inner self figure makes itself known to the therapist, it often "serves as a guide for the therapist and the patient."

When the Self appears directly in either a dream or active imagination, it is an unmistakable moment. But don't talk yourself into believing that the voice you hear is the Self. There are many tricksters lurking in the unconscious with promises of wealth, fame, and power. In that light, remember the story from the Bible of Satan taking Jesus up above the city, offering him all that he could see. Encountering the Self is like falling in love, you'll know when it happens. I would caution that it is wise to remember that even the Self emerges from our psyche. While it is beyond our ability to comprehend, it is not necessarily God with a capital "G" or even a god, but simply the only structure we have available through which we can perceive divinity.

Working within structured methods such as the two I've previously mentioned (i.e., chakra power animals and path-walking), you are less prone to excesses of inflation and depression than simply engaging with figures from the unconscious. As such, such methods are especially useful when one is just beginning to try active imagination. Even within normal unstructured active imagination, however, one can build support structures that are available when necessary. For example, you can ask figures in active imagination if they will be willing to protect you from harm or notify you when there is danger. You can set up some simple warning between you and the unconscious figure; for example, a physical action like your arm jerking upwards. Or you can simply let the inner figure use its imagination (if that doesn't seem too inappropriate a pun here).

In this paper, I've developed at some length the concept that we each possess personified emotional components within. It is, of course, an article of our own belief system, as to how we regard such figures. I am presenting them as possibilities for change, whether they appear in dreams, in projection, or in active imagination.

Most important, we must retain our own responsibility in dealing with them, and not automatically defer to their judgement.

[This article was adapted from material in Robin Robertson, *The Shadow's Gift* (Nicolas-Hays, 2011).]

REFERENCES

(1) Janet Dallett, "Active Imagination in Practice," in *Jungian Analysis,* Murray Stein, Editor (La Salle, Illinois: Open Court Publishing), p. 176.

(2) Richard Noll, "Multiple Personality, Dissociation, and C. G. Jung's Complex Theory", *The Journal of Analytical Psychology, Vol. 34, No. 4* (October 1989), p. 364. Emphasis in original.

(3) Théodore Flournoy, *Spiritism and Psychology* (New York and London: Harper & Brothers, 1911), p. 57.

(4) C. G. Jung, "The Transcendent Function" (1916), *Collected Works, Vol. 8: The Structure and Dynamics of the Psyche, 2nd edition* (Princeton: Princeton University Press, Bollingen Series, 1969), par. 193.

(5) Block quote and quote in next paragraph by Frederick Myers, in Sonu Shamdasani, "Automatic Writing and the Discovery of the Unconscious", *Spring 54* (1993), p. 114.

(6) Pierre Janet, *L'Automatisme Psychologigue* (Paris: Alcan, 1889), p. 135; translated by Sonu Shamdasani, in "Automatic Writing and the Discovery of the Unconscious", p. 119.

(7) Quotation in Sonu Shamdasani, "Automatic Writing and the Discovery of the Unconscious", p. 118.

(8) block quote and following quote: Ira Progoff, *The Image of an Oracle* (New York: Helix Press Book, Garrett Publications, 1964), pp. 357-8.

(9) Henry Reed, *Channeling Your Higher Self* (Virginia Beach, VA: A.R.E. Press, 2007), p. 199.

(10) Barbara Hannah, "Active Imagination", unpublished record of a talk given in Zurich on Sept. 25, 1967 at a Special Lecture Series for the C. G. Jung Educational Center of Houston, Texas, p. 7.

(11) Joan Chodorow, ed., *Jung on Active Imagination* (Princeton: Princeton University Press, 1997), p. 3.

(12) For more on projection as an inherent part of perception, see Robin Robertson, "The Mote in Your Eye." (1998). *Psychological Perspectives #36.*

(13) Joan Chodorow, ed., *Jung on Active Imagination,* p. 2.

(14) Janet Dallett, "Active Imagination in Practice," in *Jungian Analysis,* Murray Stein, Editor (La Salle, Illinois: Open Court Publishing), Dallett, " p. 180.

(15) David Fideler, Notes for Manius of Samaria, *The Life of Proclus,* David Fideler, editor (Grand Rapids: Phanes Press, 1986), p. 61.

(16) Richard Noll, "Multiple Personality, Dissociation, and C. G. Jung's Complex Theory", p. 365.

Made in the USA
Monee, IL
04 November 2026

67375843R10167